THE
BUFFALO
SAGA

THE

BUFFALO

SAGA

A STORY FROM WORLD WAR II U.S. ARMY

92ND INFANTRY DIVISION

KNOWN AS THE BUFFALO SOLDIERS

James Harden Daugherty

SYMBOLIC IMPORTANCE

It is the desire of the author that this book "The Buffalo Saga" first publication date be January 20, 2009 or as close as possible to the swearing in date of the 44th president of the United States of America. The purpose being to establish a symbolic connection between this date and the benevolent thrust as described in The Buffalo Saga.

The words to ring out are "Benevolent Thrust For Perpetuity"

FOUR OF MY PERSONAL MIRACLES

MIRACLE I
Senior Soldier had been shot by a sniper. Sam had injured his back. The author was okay. Many shells had fallen close to us. We had to leave this area. We walked through fires of hell as though we were already dead.

MIRACLE II
Fellow soldiers stared at me in amazement. A fragment of steel sparkling, in the sunlight, was wedged in my steel helmet. The piece of shrapnel had punched a hole in my helmet liner and stopped 1/4 of an inch from penetrating my head. I still have this helmet.

MIRACLE III
The order had arrived. About three hundred men, in the dark of the night, should walk up this mountain, capture an enemy soldier and return. There he was—sitting behind a machine gun. He was guarding a cave of sleeping enemy soldiers. He did not fire his weapon. I captured him and withdrew down the mountain. Why did he not shoot me?

MIRACLE IV   We had taken hills X, Y, and Z. We were ready to swoop down into the valley and capture a small town. I heard our supporting artillery fire coming from our rear. One shell fell short. It was a direct hit on our company post, where our captain, I and six other men were assembled. Five men died almost immediately. The captain was severely wounded. I did not have a scratch. Why?

These are some of my personal miracles that I am sharing.

To order additional copies of this book, contact:
Xlibris Corporation
1-888-795-4274
www.Xlibris.com
Orders@Xlibris.com
42883

CONTENTS

In memory of my parents, George and Lillie Daugherty, and my parents-in-law, Wilbur and Blanche Ward. To my beloved wife, Dorothy. To my children, Derek, Don, David, Daniel, and Diane. To my grandchildren, Ramsey, Damani, Tiffany, Chase, Chelsey, Taylor, and Nicholas. To my extended family, the Daughertys, the Williams, the Wards, and the Jacksons. To all persons who have been in wars and all families who have been touched by wars.

ACKNOWLEDGMENTS

I owe my thanks to my wife, Dorothy, who put a great deal of time and effort into this book from start to completion and offered support and encouragement.

PREFACE

At nineteen years of age, I was drafted into the United States Army, during World War II. I am a Black American. This meant that I must fight for a country that regarded me as an individual with no rights in the United States of America that white Americans were bound to respect. Having received my letter of induction, I struggled with a vexing question, "Why should I fight abroad for freedom even as I am denied freedom at home?"

I was discharged from the United States Army in February 1946. I wrote *The Buffalo Saga* in 1947. For the next several years, I tried to get it published, but I was unsuccessful. During my retirement, I was inspired to pick up the manuscript again. This is my story. I continue to see it as a worthwhile endeavor that I should pursue.

INTRODUCTION

Thursday, April 17, 1947

I talked with Kev today. We talked of men and war—men who fought and men who died. Many men had the same experiences that we had. However, there was something different about the men of whom we spoke. They were Black Americans, and Kev and I were two of these Black Americans who had survived the devastation of war. It's good to talk with a friend who has shared the same experiences and hardships as you have. It is a good feeling—something too satisfying to present with man's feeble words.

I guess you wonder how this conversation started between Kev and me. Well, I was at the university today, Howard University. I was in the locker room of the gymnasium when Mr. Barry, a friend and now a professor, approached. I spoke to him and danced about as if I were boxing with him. Mr. Barry turned to Kev who was standing nearby and said, "Isn't this the happiest fellow you have ever seen?"

I placed my hand on Barry's shoulder and chuckled. "I'm still alive, why shouldn't I be happy?" Mr. Barry looked at me in his usual wise manner as if to say, what is his story now?

Then I said, "Say, Kev, tell him what I mean"; and as the fellows say, that started it. When I arrived home that evening, some irresistible force inside me kept insisting, *Write about it, write about it, write about it.*

CHAPTER ONE

SAILING

Well, this is it! The fellows have started up that much-dreaded thing called a gangplank. "By the way, Sam, what is today?"

Sam responded, "Today is Thursday, September 21, 1944, and don't forget it because before long, you will probably realize that it was one of the most important days in your life."

Sam was the fellow beside me in line. I had met him in the army about fifteen months before we sailed. Sam was twenty-one years old, intelligent, sincere, dependable, and a person I loved as a brother. His home and family were in one of the Southern States. He had attended college and worked prior to being inducted into the army. He was about five feet ten inches tall, slender, and had a rather quiet, settled look about him. He seemed shy and friendly. He was hardly the type of fighting man one sees in the movies, but looks are so deceiving as I found out later. As Sam had said, this was one of the most important days in my life, and I would never forget it. Little did I realize the fear, hardships, and unforgettable horror that we, as fighting "Black men" from the United States of America, were going to experience.

Just think, when the war between Poland and Germany started,
I was sixteen years old. It seemed like a far-fetched story to me.
It was something to hear about on the radio and to read about in
the newspapers. I never thought that I would be so involved in this
absurdity that really wasn't absurd. It's like being wrapped up in
some weird dream. You know you are having a bad dream; you
try to wake up, but you can't. Have you ever been in that sort of
situation? Here today; there tomorrow. Where am I anyway? Oh
well, why worry about it? I am what they call a Colored man, so
at least I won't have to fight. This may be a fighting outfit, but
we will never see action. I bet they will give us picks and shovels
before we leave the boat. So what! I won't condemn it. I'm not
one of those who is fooled into wanting to fight anyhow. Why
should I, or any of us, want to sacrifice so much? We have been
mistreated an awful lot, and things aren't getting any better. In
fact, these people are doing it right in this outfit instead of trying
to build some morale. I don't understand Americans' concept
of life, pushing a man around and still expecting him to fight
for them. They have a nerve to call it "giving us a chance." A
chance to prove that I can fight! That's for those who don't feel
they are as good as the next man. I know better.

Some were fooled into asking for the chance to fight—even
demanded it. However, most of those who did the asking and
demanding knew that they would not do the fighting directly;
but that some other poor souls, many years younger than they
would, do the "bullet stopping" and the "limb losing." Don't
worry; those American folks will stop kidding themselves and
the Black folks about giving somebody a chance to fight. You
know, the American officials seem to think that by making
believe they are giving the Colored folks a chance; the Colored
folks will be eager to prove that they can fight and will gladly
give their all. Some will, and some won't. At the same time,
they can't be allowed to perform too good and accomplish

too much; for then, the officials in control will not be able to completely enjoy their superiority complex and who would they then use as a scapegoat. I believe that many of the officials were good, wholesome citizens; but at this time, the evil ones are dominating, and it is of them I speak. Think about it. It is a wonderful thing, an honor, and a duty for a man to fight for his country; but if attempts are made to motivate him by trickery, deceit, and untruths, he will never feel that he is fighting for things that are supposedly his. "Say, Sam, what time is it? We have been on this boat long enough for it to start moving somewhere." It seems as though these words aroused the crew to action for suddenly, the anchor was pulled, and we set sail.

Our quarters were in a small stuffy area of a Liberty ship. We bunked three high and two wide, with a small aisle to pass between the hammocklike bunks. I am certain that I have a true conception of how sardines feel.

After four days at sea, everyone was tired of watching those furious blue-and-white-capped mounds, which seemed like an endless number of vibrations. Many were the days that we spent cooped up on that small Liberty ship, seeing the same faces, same deck, same miles and miles of water. Usually, during the day, we would have a few calisthenics to make sure that our muscles would not be allowed to become too lazy.

Being a fisherman, I spent many hours watching to see if I could discover any sort of marine life. Many times, I saw a flying fish emerge from the water and then dive back into the ocean again. Once, I saw a stingray near the surface. My greatest thrills occurred when I observed schools of porpoises, breaking and leaping from the water. I see now why people claim so often that they have seen sea dragons because the leaping porpoises at a distance appear to form a dragonlike tail.

From time to time, classes were held at night in the art of map reading and the use of the compass. Weapons were cleaned frequently, and much time was spent listening to the radio in hopes that the war might, by some twist of fate, end before we reached the front. Chowtime, the moment that most soldiers looked forward to, had become a very unpleasant task. Most of the men were seasick from the rolling and tossing of the ship. To add to this, the food for the most part was poorly prepared. Very little of the food actually went through the process of digestion for it usually came up the same way it went down. To make matters worse, our arms were still being used as pincushions. Some more typhus shots they called them.

The restlessness of the men soon began to show itself. One soldier, whom most considered a bully and who got along with very few individuals, struck one of the men on the head with a steel helmet, after the two had argued over something too insignificant to mention. The injured soldier, who was considered a quiet fellow who bothered no one, without any apparent show of emotion, pressed a handkerchief to his bloody scalp and walked off to the ship's dispensary where the doctor put several stitches of catgut in his head. Many men felt uneasy and hatred toward the soldier who had struck one of his own comrades in such a manner. He had struck, not because of what the other man had done to him, but because of the miserable surroundings in which he had been placed. The quiet fellow, however, did not let the matter go by as easily as he had seemed to; for with the same amount of apathy he had displayed in walking to the dispensary, he returned in the same manner, obtained a Coca-Cola bottle and struck his assailant on the head. This called for more catgut. Both men were disciplined, and the incident was dropped.

That night, I lay on my bunk unable to go to sleep because of the shrill tone of an ocarina that had been issued by the Red Cross and was now being enjoyed by some musically inclined GIs. Across the aisle in the dark, two more soldiers were just as unhappy about the presence of the musician and were scheming how they could rid themselves of this peace disturber. This is the plan they hatched. One of them would locate the exact position of the musician; then he would return to his friend and inform him of the location. The friend would quietly toss a Coca-Cola bottle in the direction of the musician. So out went the scout to locate the enemy. In the meanwhile, the friend became impatient with the return of his scout, so he threw the bottle in the direction of the sound. A thud; then a scream was heard, but it was not the musician who was struck; it was the unfortunate scout. This called for still more catgut.

For the next three days, I observed the two recent victims of Coke bottles with their patches, convalescing on the deck. Coca-Cola bottles were considered dangerous weapons, and orders were that they should be returned to the post exchange as soon as they were empty.

One morning, as the golden sunshine peeped from its soft white sheets, I was awakened by the mad rushing of men, up the iron steps of the ship, and yelling about land and good old Mother Earth. I joined the rush to see some of this good old rock and soil. Yep, there it was, real down to earth, earth. Some called it Spain; others said it was Africa, but the sailors aboard the ship said it was the Rock of Gibraltar, and that we would soon be entering the Straits of Gibraltar. I had heard much about the Rock. It was the British stronghold in the Mediterranean area and had withstood all of the bombing that the Nazis could dish out. We must have fiddled around in these straits for several days, slowly poking along as if we were in no hurry at all.

Behind this rocklike island, one could see the coast of Spain and, on the right, the coast of Africa. It wasn't long before we drew near Sicily and the coast of Italy. As we passed between the two bodies of land, Italian peasants rowed near the ship in skiffs. They yelled out to us, "Paisano! Paisano! Cigarettes! Cigarettes!" They threw green limes to the soldiers who stood along the rails, and in return, the soldiers threw packages of cigarettes into the sea. There was a mad scramble of skiffs for the floating packages of cigarettes.

Next, we entered the Port of Naples. One of the most beautiful and picturesque ports in the world with old Mount Vesuvius magnificently evil, yet a striking piece of natural beauty when seen from the distance. Some say that when it is not admired enough, it goes into childlike tantrums and belches fire and destruction upon the native inhabitants. The convoy anchored and remained in the Port of Naples until that night. Then very early in the morning, the ships set sail again.

In the late evening, we anchored at Leghorn, our port of debarkation upon this foreign shore where we would do battle. What a strange feeling it was when my feet touched once again the earth. As I walked about, it seemed as though the ground was playing tricks on me. I had become accustomed to walking on a ship that constantly rolled from side to side, and now this still mass of Mother Earth, below my feet, disturbed my equilibrium. Of course, I was not alone, for all the soldiers appeared to be newborn babies who had just learned to walk and were still not confident of their ability to travel about. The sailors, on board the ship, practically rolled with laughter, across the deck, upon witnessing this scene of a group of full-grown men, trying to walk. At this point, it occurred to me the reasons for such expressions used by sailors such as getting your sea legs or getting your land legs.

CHAPTER TWO

PREPARATION FOR THE FRONT

Thirty days we had spent on that Liberty ship. Just about one month ago, we were in the United States of America, and now, we were in Italy with miles and miles of ocean, separating us from home. It was beginning to get dark, and big army trucks were rolling onto the dock. We loaded aboard, took one look at our dear ship, and then sped off in a long convoy of trucks to new mentally degrading and physically destroying situations. After traveling about ten miles, we finally reached our bivouac area. Immediately after unloading from the truck, we left our packs and rifles in a prearranged spot. Then we proceeded to a mess hall constructed of wood and received some hot victuals in our mess kits.

Many troops were stationed in this area, and as I emerged from the chow line, I observed them sitting about on the ground eating. Also, in amazement, I observed the citizens of this foreign land, boys and girls, men and women, young and old, passing among the soldiers begging for any leftovers that the soldiers might have left over in their mess kits. Many of these unfortunate people carried several large tin cans, one for any coffee they could beg, one for vegetables, another for bread, and another for meat. They did not eat the food as they collected it, for many were getting dinner for their families at home or storing food for future hardships. Many soldiers deliberately asked for more than they could eat so that they would have some left for their new friends. To see the thankful expressions upon the faces of these people as they were given the food was more than reward enough for a soldier. A soldier on foreign shores is a lonely person, and any friend that he may gain is indeed an experience of pleasure. The loneliness felt by the Black soldier is even greater and more empty; and this, together with the many devaluations that he had received in his native land, only served to give him more understanding of these people's suffering and ever eager to gain their friendships.

After eating, we pitched our small pup tents and sat around, discussing the trip and what lay ahead. The night was clear, but dark. Many stars shown in the heavens, but no moon was in sight. Practically, every group of fellows had a small light that they had made by filling a can with sand, then poured enough kerosene into the sand to dampen minute particles of stone and quartz. To this, a lighted match was touched, and a steady small flame was provided to illuminate the small patch of darkness, in which each group of soldiers sat. Some played cards, some shot crap, some talked of the future, some sat silent just thinking, but from each group there seemed to glow rays of security and protection that only a feeling of being a part of a little group can send forth.

In a group of soldiers such as this, you will always find someone who will immediately begin to explore his new surroundings. Of course, I was very happy when several soldiers made it their business to visit several neighboring farmhouses and returned with a large bag of chestnuts. Immediately, a debate began as to whether or not we could eat these things. There was no doubt about it in my mind as to their being edible, for my mother had frequently brought them home when I was a child, and I had always enjoyed roasting and eating hot chestnuts. We quickly gathered up some wood and made a blazing fire. The chestnuts were put in some of the finished burning, but hot, glowing wood chunks. The chestnuts signified that they were done by resounding with a sharp crack as the tasty meat expanded in its shell. Some anxious GIs experienced the same unpleasant results that the cat did when the cat and the monkey were engaged in a chestnut feast. They burned their fingers from handling the hot chestnuts.

What would you do if there were not some curious fellows who went to meddle and returned with some chestnuts to roast? Can you see the importance of this small act among men about to fight in a war? Here we are, sitting and standing around a glowing fire, telling jokes and stories, singing, and eating hot chestnuts. We had forgotten about war. Our brains were relaxing. The brain needs just a little recreation to heal the damage that has been done by stress and tension, and here it was, being provided by a bag of chestnuts. I dozed off that night in my pup tent, quite satisfied that I had spent a pleasant evening; and Sam, in his half, seemed the same.

We remained in this area for about two weeks, readying our equipment, running a few dry-run combat problems, and listening to tales from soldiers who had been to the front. Then one day, in the late afternoon, we got the word. In about two hours, we would be moving out. We packed most of our personal belongings in duffel bags and attached our names to the bags. To the front, we would carry our weapons, an entrenchment tool, a canteen, a cartridge belt, a first-aid packet, a trench knife, a bayonet, one blanket, a gas mask, a mess kit, a raincoat, a pack in which most of the paraphernalia was to be rolled and the "clothes on our backs." The "clothes on our backs" consisted of heavy woolen socks, high-top rubber boots that laced up, and had felt pads on the inside, a suit of long underwear, a pair of woolen pants, a woolen shirt, a high-neck woolen sweater, a field jacket, a woolen cap, a helmet liner, and a steel helmet. The woolen pants and shirts were the same type as those a soldier wears when he goes on pass in the States.

I said, "Um-mm, Sam, trucks again; it appears as though these army trucks are quite essential in this war. I hope we keep riding and don't start walking all over the world."

Sam replied, "Caution, dear friend; this is still the infantry, and the infantry still walks. What you are doing is known in educational circles as wishful thinking."

As we loaded on the trucks, I said to Sam, "Brother, you may be right, so I guess I had better make an extra effort to enjoy this ride like a child makes an extra effort to enjoy its ice-cream cone."

It didn't take our battalion long to "load on," and then we were off. "Say, Sam, these guys can really wheel these trucks, can't they?"

"Yep," answered Sam, "but I'm in no hurry to go where they are going. I feel like I'm rushing to my own funeral."

I imagine we rode for about an hour before these imitation busses ceased burning gas. We were not an hours ride from the front to begin with at the speed these trucks had been traveling, but much-extra driving was done to prevent the enemy spies from knowing just exactly in which direction the troops were traveling.

The trucks stopped in a heavily wooded area, and we unloaded. Before we could get off the road good, the trucks had turned off the road and left as though this section of land was going to cave in or something. "Sam, did you see how those guys got out of here! This must not be a very nice place to be."

"Well," Sam said, "don't worry your curious brain about it because we are leaving also on foot."

Sam was right; the group of soldiers, farther up the road, were moving forward about three hundred yards and turning off into the woods. We walked into the woods about seven hundred yards and stopped. Here, we received enough C rations for one meal. It was rather late in the evening, about dusk and time to eat, so naturally, everyone proceeded to do just that. We were to pick up our ammunition here, remain until darkness set in, and then move out to the front on foot. That expression "on foot" makes me boil. What this army needs is some automatic shoes that just lift the feet up and put them down again.

Just before darkness set in, our platoon guide returned with enough ammunition for each man to load his rifle with one clip that is about seven bullets per man. We also received a hand grenade for every two men. "Say, Sam, maybe they are celebrating the Fourth of July early in the States this year and have run out of powder."

In a sarcastic manner, Sam replied, "We will have to cooperate very closely with the hand grenade. You pull the pin, and I'll throw the thing."

Another soldier chirped in, "Some of these fellows will use these seven rounds just from seeing things and having bad dreams tonight."

The platoon guide, who felt as though he was being blamed, said, "All right, hold your horses; you can get ammunition from the fortunate fellows you relieve at the front."

When all signs of daylight had withdrawn from the heavens, we set out walking in columns of twos and about five yards apart. In the far distance, we could hear the rumble of cannons. The night had become cloudy and very dark—an excellent night for moving into position. The pace of the route-step march was very rapid, causing one to actually run at times in order to close gaps. Occasionally, we stopped for short-rest periods. This had been going on for an hour now, and most of us had begun to perspire freely although the night was cool.

After two hours of rapid walking, our muscles began to show signs of fatigue, and the men began to grumble. After many days aboard ship, their legs were not in top condition. My back and shoulder muscles had become very pained from the pack. The constant bouncing up and down of the load had begun to irritate a small section of my back. Soon, it began to rain slightly; and later, this turned into a steady pitter-patter of raindrops.

After three and a half hours of walking, the column came to a halt. Boy, was I glad. My whole body was completely fatigued. It seemed as though I couldn't take another step. "Well, Sam, this must be the place."

"If it isn't the place, you will have to carry me the rest of the way," Sam said. We were among several groups of houses, and I could see several soldiers moving about. We soon learned that this was only the command post where the company commander and his staff would remain.

In a few seconds, a guide joined us who was to take our platoon to its position. Slowly we moved out. My fatigued muscles had begun to ache, and the steady rainfall had helped to make my pack heavier. As we emerged from the town, I spotted a sharply rising hill that was about five hundred feet in height and was dug out in a rounded steplike pattern. I later discovered that this pattern was used to cultivate olive trees.

As the guide started up the hill, I cursed to myself in disgust. Angry at whoever was responsible for my tired feet and aching back, angry at whoever was responsible for my being here, angry because I did not feel that those responsible for my being here were suffering with me.

With every step up this muddy slope, I glanced ahead, hoping that the guide would say this is it. Just as I was about to throw my pack from my back and defy the whole world to make me take another step, I heard a command, "Halt," and then silence. Everyone froze in his tracks. Then I heard the word "fox." Our guide replied, "Hunt."

The voice in the dark replied, "Move on." We had reached our positions. The password was "foxhunt." The one who challenges the trespasser yells, "Halt" and then gives half of the password "fox." If the trespasser cannot respond with "hunt," he will be shot down in his tracks. I said to myself, *Soldiers, this is really business; don't ever forget the password. The password would change every night. Tomorrow, it would be ball game.*

Our guide pointed out the position of foxholes. The platoon sergeant said, "Just pick a foxhole, and get in it." All along the muddy hill, the wet, unshaven, battle-worn and tested soldiers were moving out of holes, and new beginners were taking their places. As I stumbled along the hill, a soldier said to me, "Here, fellow, you can have my hole." He looked tired, but very happy to be leaving this hill.

I said, "Thanks," and he moved off. I looked at this hole dug into the earth and then, without thinking, threw in my backpack. To my surprise, I heard a resounding splash as though someone had thrown a large rock into a river. I thought, *Well, there will not be any sleeping in this foxhole tonight.* I reached into the foxhole with the end of my bayonet and recovered my pack. It was soaked with muddy water. Then I looked around to seek another foxhole in which to spend the night.

Silhouetted against the dark night, I could distinguish through the raindrops the outline of a small house. I thought, *This is where I will spend the night.* The house was only forty feet away, so with a few hops and skips; I was there. I had no difficulty getting inside because only three sides of the house were standing, and half of the roof was missing. Inside the walls, there were six or seven other soldiers who must have also thrown their packs into this same muddy, water-filled foxhole. Most of the smooth, hard spots had been taken by them, so I assumed a one-third lying, one-third sitting, and one-third standing position on a pile of rocks and spent the rest of the night half asleep, twisting and turning with rain, dripping upon me from half of a roof.

CHAPTER THREE

FIRST TEN DAYS ON THE FRONT

As soon as it was light enough to see clearly, I began to think about seeking a foxhole to make my residence during the time that I would be on this hill. How did we happen to have this hill anyhow? Well, the story goes like this. While we were still in the States, one of our sister regiments, the 370th Infantry Regiment, had already arrived in Italy with an artillery outfit and tank outfit. They had spearheaded the Fifth Army's Arno River drive and were the first outfit to cross the Arno River. After they crossed the Arno, they pushed on to take a town called Lucca. The 370th Infantry Regiment steadily drove the Germans across the flat coastal plains of Italy. This small hill was one of the greatest obstacles in their path and the first strongpoint of the feared Gothic Line of German fortification. Behind this hill lay many more hills and mountains of even greater height to form the north Apennine Mountains. After this, there was the Po Valley and then the Alps; from here on until they could break through into the Po Valley, the fighting would consist of mountain fighting.

When the 370th Infantry Regiment reached this first series of mountains, they realized that they must take at least some of these mountains, if not all of them, or else be at the complete mercy of German artillery fire. This small hill was one of those that the 370th Infantry Regiment had taken. In doing so, they had paid dearly in dead and wounded. After taking this hill, they dug their foxholes and were sitting tight, waiting for the next move.

What was left of the 370th Infantry Regiment after the push across the Arno River, the capture of Lucca, and the smashing of the first strongpoint of the Gothic Line was a proud outfit. They had established a fine record as fighting men, and since they were an all-Black outfit, they had received much publicity in the States in both the black-and-white newspapers. Before we even left the States, we had read the great accomplishments of the 370th Infantry Regiment. For the moment, the American officials had settled the foolish arguments as to whether or not the Black soldier would make a good combat man. The 370th Combat Team had done so well that the 371st Infantry Regiment and the rest of the division were now moving into action. Yes, the 370th Infantry Regiment, composed of Black soldiers, had done well; but this only aroused some envious American officials to action. All along, they had yelled and screamed that the Negro was only fit for labor. Now they were eating their words. They must find new means, new schemes to prove what they had said. So began the lowest form of shameful acts in history; as some, but not all, politicians sought to prove that some of the bravest men who had ever worn the uniform of the United States Army were not courageous. These politicians never succeeded in lowering the courage and brave deeds of the Black soldier, but they did succeed in lowering the morale and faith of many a good American in the so-called American way of life. These politicians succeeded in giving comfort to the enemy and in aiding in the death of many a brave man who fought for his country.

So you see the greatest obstacle before the 92nd Infantry Division was not the German Army, not the mountains of Italy, not the mud, not the rain and the cold; but the greatest obstacle and handicap was the foolish political games of those who would go to any extent to advance their self-interests. These politicians considered human lives as being mere matches that they could strike whenever they so desired as long as the burning of these bodies satisfied their desires. The sad fact about the whole situation is that the gullible American citizens, who supported these politicians, never realized that if it had become necessary that these individuals would sacrifice them in the same manner as they had sacrificed the Buffalo Soldiers. Many of the American officials were fair in their dealings with the Black American soldier. The involvement of the American Army officers, if any, is not clear.

Such bitterness. I must not let it control me. Yet I must not destroy this bitterness for it motivates me to action and opens my eyes. As I glanced about this hill, it did not seem that important to me; but when I thought of the stream of blood that had run down its gullies and had soaked into its rich soil, I knew that we all must treasure and protect this hill in debt to those whose flesh passed into its surface.

I continued to survey the side of this hill and spotted what appeared to be a chipmunk, poking its head out of a hole. After closer observation, I found that it was not a chipmunk, but my good friend, Sam. I went over to Sam's hole to see if there was room enough for two. It didn't take me long to see that the foxhole wasn't even fit for one. Sam and I decided to dig another hole, just at the end of the olive grove. This gave us a good view of the valley in front of us and the next hill across the valley. *The enemy wouldn't be able to spot us*, we thought, *because of the olive trees*. After we had been digging, for about half an hour, three soldiers moved a machine gun into position about twenty yards to our left and began to dig in. Sam and I felt pretty good when we saw that. Sam said, "Those Germans had better not try to come up this side of the hill."

I agreed with Sam. Then I said to him, "You know, Sam, I haven't seen any signs of food today. Suppose I run over here and find the platoon sergeant and see if I can get some chow." Sam nodded to indicate an okay, and off I went in search of some grub.

I had just rounded the curved slope of the hill when I heard something streak through the air and almost, at the same time, an ear-dulling explosion. Immediately, I knew it was a mortar shell, for I had heard them many times during combat training. Five or six shells must have fallen before the fire was lifted, and everyone seemed to fall where I had just left Sam, digging the foxhole. I lay prone upon the ground for about three minutes to see if any more shells were going to fall. Then I glanced up and down the sides of the hill. I could see anxious faces, peering from the foxholes. I was about to get up and see how Sam made out when I heard some quick footsteps, moving toward me. Yes, it was Sam, looking very much like he had seen a ghost.

He said without even breaking his pace, "Come on; let's get out of here."

So Sam and I moved around the side of the hill to a position where we knew the enemy could not see us. This spot was near the old house I had slept in, and near it were conveniently dug two foxholes about four yards apart. Sam jumped in one foxhole, and I took the other one. Sam must have sat in this foxhole five minutes before he recovered fully enough to say anything. Then he called to me to come over and to join him, and he would tell me what had happened.

When he began to talk, his voice was still a little unsteady. The first thing he said was, "Those Jerries can drop those mortars in your hip pockets. The first shell was a little short of my hole and the next one a little over. I figured the next one would be right in there, so I jumped out of my foxhole and took cover in an old-enemy fortification to the rear. The fellows setting up the machine guns made the same sort of move. We were none too quick either, for when the smoke and dust from the next four shells had cleared away, both of the newly prepared holes had been hit directly. The sides were caved in and a small bit of smoke crept from within. Brother, I really came close to digging my own grave."

So there it was our first hot-combat experience. And as we both sat there, looking at each other and thinking of what had just happened, we knew that we were really sitting ducks. The enemy was looking down on our heads.

The next nine days were spent on this hill, among the olive groves, ducking artillery, and mortar shells. The casualties were relatively few in number, but each was a dear buddy. Every night, some unfortunate soldiers were sent on patrol to contact the enemy. This sort of tension and anxiety slowly drives men crazy. That is why we looked up early one morning and saw cleanly dressed soldiers in rough-dry uniforms, moving into our positions. Yes, we were getting off this hill. They named it California for tactical reasons. Now we could shave, take showers, and put on some clothes that were not packed with mud. Maybe, we could even go to the Red Cross Club, get haircuts, and write letters home. Boy, just think, we can stroll around town with our chests out. Real, live-combat soldiers, just back from the front. But, best of all, we could get several good-night's rest without worrying about someone sneaking upon us to blast a hole in our bodies or a sergeant poking his head in our holes and telling us that tonight was our night to go on patrol.

Already we were rolling into town in a convoy of trucks. Our first stop was at a portable shower, then to a bivouac area where we ate a hot meal, pitched our tents, and lie down to rest. Yes, we were off the front. Suddenly, out of the blue, we heard the booming voice of our first sergeant. "Mail call, mail call!" Everyone rushed toward the first sergeant. All sparkling eyes were upon him. Every Buffalo Soldier of Company I was eagerly awaiting to hear his name called, so he could grasp that letter or package from home. Just to hear from a friend or a loved one from the shores of America was fantastic. After many minutes of stressful waiting, my name was called. It wasn't only a letter but an assortment of cookies and a local African American newspaper. To top this off, there was a copy of a letter to my mom and dad from the United States government. This letter read, "Congratulations, your son has been awarded the Combat Infantryman Badge. This is only for infantry soldiers who have completed combat missions. Infantrymen take great pride in wearing this badge." The letter dated 15 April 1945 read for the most part as follows:

Dear Parents,

Your son, Private First Class, 371st Infantry, has been awarded the Combat Infantryman Badge for his outstanding performance of duty in action against the enemy. It is with pleasure and pride that I take this means of extending to you and to him my sincere congratulations. Your son has clearly demonstrated the excellent soldierly qualities, which are in keeping with the highest traditions of the military service.

Sincerely yours,
371st Infantry
Commanding

My mom and dad expressed how proud they were of me and spread the news to my two brothers, relatives, and friends. That night, I lay down to sleep with a special glow.

CHAPTER FOUR

THE SERCHIO VALLEY

"Say, Sam! Sam! Wake up, man! The fellows are pulling down their tents, and someone said they are issuing ammunition down in Company M," I said.

Sam replied, "What! No! They can't be; we just got here."

Yes, as Sam had said, we just got here. Everyone had settled down for two or three days of rest after spending their first ten days on the front in wet, cold, muddy foxholes and eating B rations. We thought this was tough; but, brother, we didn't know. Before, we just sat in our "pig holes," ducked occasional shells, and ever so often went on night patrol to let the enemy get a little target practice. Headquarters said we were doing this to measure the enemies weren't sneaking away. Believe me; they were still there. The next move wouldn't be so trifle; for this time, we were going to take a few mountains.

The order finally reached our company. The first sergeant told us to pull down our tents, roll our packs, and report by platoons to the supply tent for ammunition. Several minutes later, a convoy of trucks rolled into the area. When you see those big trucks swing in line, you feel sort of good, sort of thrilled; for you know that you are involved in something big, something important; but then, a shudder creeps over you, and fear tingles your spine, and you realize you might get killed; you might be blown to bits; you might lose an arm, a leg. Oh, you wish you were back home in a warm house, eating a good meal, seeing a young lady. You sort of wish you would get shot, nothing serious, just enough to get you back to the States where you would be a hero with a purple heart.

Then you are angry. Why am I here anyhow, doggone it? A sharp command broke up everyone's daydreaming.

"Load up!" The order came from the captain in a sharp, clear, commanding tone. We loaded on, and the trucks began to roll. Soon, a cold rain began to fall; and when it fell, it fell on us. The trucks didn't have canvas tops on them because it was against safety regulations for trucks to be covered when troops are on the move to the front. Can you picture what it is like to see a group of men riding in an open truck for five or six hours, with cold raindrops dripping down their backs, with darkness creeping from the heavens, and with the temperatures dropping. Raincoats! Why don't you, soldiers, put on your raincoats? Ha! That's a joke. We have them on, but it isn't long before the cold on the outside and the warmth from the bodies causes large drops of moisture to condense on the interior lining of the raincoat, like moisture does on the warm inside of the windowpane when it is cold outside. If only we were going someplace where we could stand by a fire and get dry. But no! The only fire we will get near is the fire from Jerry's merciless machine gun and 88mm artillery, but that's all right, we will make him even warmer.

The trucks finally came to a halt. From now on out, it would be on foot. Right now, walking in the rain was much better than riding in those trucks, that is, if we can walk because I was cold, numb, and stiff all over, and I imagined that everyone else felt the same. One good thing, no one would have to worry about getting wet because they were already soaked from head to toe.

After walking for about a mile, we came into a small town located in a very hilly area. To everyone's surprise, we learned that we would sleep here in real houses for the rest of the night, but no fires. The heat from your body will dry your clothes, and the combined heat from many sleeping bodies on the floor of the same room. When I got inside the house, I was so relieved to get out of the rain that I forgot about the cold. I bedded my blankets on the floor, and I was so tired that when I hit the floor, it felt like a rubber-foam mattress reinforced with horsehair and innersprings. Two seconds later, I was in a deep sleep, wet clothes, and all.

The next day, they let us build fires. We cleaned and oiled our rifles, checked our ammunition, and set our equipment in order. We cooked a good meal, and most of the tension that had been present eased out of sight. The boys began to joke, to smile, and to know that life was still worth living.

Suddenly, our platoon leader strolled into the room with a dead-serious look on his face, and everyone knew that things would soon be jumping. He informed us that about dusk, we would set out on foot for a jumping-off point. We were to remain at this point until five o'clock in the morning, which would be about daybreak, and then launch an attack to take as much ground from the enemy as we could, then dig in. This statement came from him: "The best thing that you can do is to pray that none of those bullets has your name on it." I knew that people said things like this in the movies, but here was a man in a real-life situation, using such words of chance.

I looked around me, and it was gone. It was gone. Those happy smiles, those lively men; all that was left was a dead, dull silence. We knew tomorrow, early in the morning; some of us would die; some of us would be wounded. Who? Who would be fortunate? Who would be unfortunate? What would decide? Who would decide? Was it a matter of pure chance, or was there a God who would protect some, kill none, but leave others to this thing called luck or chance?

Immediately, we rolled our packs, and the rest of the day was spent in quiet conversation. About sunset, we hit the road, walking in a route-step column of twos with one column on each side of the road. After walking an hour, it began to rain, and I realized that if I had stayed wet, I would have been better off. The increasing loudness of rumbling cannons and bursting shells told us that we were very near to the front. Soon, we arrived at the base of a steep hill. Here, we were told to leave our packs by a tree. We were informed that the climb was so difficult that we would be able to carry only our weapons, ammunition, and what we actually wore. "Say, Sam, do you know what this means? We are going up into the mountains without any blankets. They must think it is summertime."

Sam said, "Don't worry; they will bring them up on mules later."

It wasn't long before I was glad that I didn't have those heavy blankets on my back. The climb required about four hours of struggling and slipping up a muddy mountain. Everyone was exhausted when we reached the jumping-off point. If the enemy had jumped over the top of the mountain, we would have been too tired to raise our rifles and fire. Orders were sent down that we were to remain here until just before daybreak and then proceed to take the next mountain on which the Jerries were firmly entrenched. I reached down to feel my bed, which of course was the ground. Nothing, but mud, oozy mud with a few leaves scattered here and there. *Leaves, leaves*, I thought.

I must gather some leaves, but everyone else had the same idea. I managed to gather enough wet leaves though to cover a small patch of ground, and then I curled up like an armadillo, pulled my raincoat over my head, and with the sound of hail and rain beating on my thin covering, I fell off to sleep to await the coming of dawn.

I was awakened by the hustle and bustle of restless men. Everyone was preparing to move. It was getting light fast, and we knew that we must move as much as possible under the cover of the early morning, hoping to catch the enemy napping. Our platoon moved off to the right to take a small hill, which contained several farmhouses. We reached the top of the mountain, staying within heavy bushes and trees to avoid being seen. Now we could look down into a shallow valley in which hovered a still, quiet mist, and then the land began to rise again until it formed a small hill. This was it. This was the hill where our platoon was going. The hill didn't look so bad, but that valley. We must cross that valley. We waited. Any moment now, our artillery would tear those hills down to make it easy for us. Then it began. *Wham! Wham! Wham!* Three shells. Three lousy shells; then it ceased. Surely, they don't call that a barrage. Why, that didn't even shake the birds out of the trees. The lieutenant told me that our squad would proceed first while the other squads covered us from this point. He pointed out the drawl that we would use as an approach. I thought, *I am the A Scout, that means that I will be first. Sam is the B Scout, so he will cover me.* Down into the valley, we moved slowly, cautiously. Over to the left, they were raising hell. Bullets were humming; mortar shells were falling, and dueling machine guns were active. I knew that the other platoons and companies were meeting stiff resistance, but not us. Things were still quiet. Up the drawl, I started, watching every tree and rock with suspicion; occasionally, I glanced to the rear to see how Sam and the rest of the squad were doing. Then the drawl ended.

In front and slightly to the rear were two houses, directly to the front and on the exact top of the hill was another house shielded by a row of hedges. I motioned to Sam to come up so that I could talk to him. The plan was for me to sneak forward and throw hand grenades into first one house and then the other, while Sam covered me. I crawled forward along the reversed slope of the hill until I was within twenty yards of the house. The distance that I had to cover was over open grass, broken only by a large granite rock. What should I do? Crawl to the rock or make a quick catlike dash across the short open spaces to the rock. In basic training, they had taught us to make a quick dash if there wasn't much firing. Up I sprang and almost dashed past the rock in my rush for dear life. Well, here I am. If anyone in the house saw me make that move then I will be a sitting duck if I pop up again. I guess I will stick here for a few minutes; maybe, they will think that this is as far as I am going. One, two, three minutes, I wasn't afraid while I was moving, but this waiting bites at your guts. I thought, *I had better move before I let fear freeze me.* Another quick dash and I was up to the house. Sam, in the meanwhile, had moved to the rock that I had just left, and the rest of the squad was concealed in the drawl.

Just above my head was a window. It did not contain glass but was barred by two swinginglike wooden doors, which were tightly shut. That was why I had approached the house from this side. If anyone opened those wooden windows to fire at me, Sam would see them and open up first. Maybe, there is an open window on the other side of the house; I could put a grenade through it, but if I move around the other side, Sam would not be able to cover me. I glanced back to the rear. There,

I saw Sam who looked very restless and not too comfortable, crouched behind this large granite rock in a patch of soggy grass. I could see that the rest of the squad was in a position to cover both of us. I motioned to Sam to join me beside the house, and he did with a burst of speed that would put any Texas jackrabbit to shame. "Say, Sam, if I crawl around to the other side of this house and stay close to the wall, no one within the house can spot me, but someone can spot me from the other house to the right. This house I want you to watch." Without hesitating, I crawled to the other side of the house, and yes, there it was an open window. Quickly, I reached into the extra canteen cover that I had fastened to my cartridge belt, grasped a grenade, pulled the pin, reached up gently, and tossed it into the window. Then I bit the dust. One, two, three seconds, and a sharp explosion pierced the air, followed by the sound of steel, tearing through wood and ricocheting off concrete walls; then silence. Damned silence, no Jerries yelling for mercy, no scared twerderskies hanging out white flags, not even a lousy roach came out. All that creeping and crawling, dashing and darting, sweating and swearing, struggling and stumbling, watching and waiting; and the joint was as empty as a crap-game clubhouse gets when someone yells that a cop is coming. Boy, was I mad. Now, I must get to the next house. I won't waste any time fooling with this one. Sam can spot me when I make a dash for it. I grasped my M1, fastened the canteen cover that held the other grenades, and ran a good thirty yards to a small outhouse located about five yards from the farmhouse. I stopped just long enough to catch a breath of air. Then I moved to an open window of the house, tossed in a grenade, and again hugged the earth. Again, hot steel filled the air, and the twang of powder bit my nostrils, but no Jerries.

Two down, and one to go. One more river to cross. Just one more farmhouse. What is this? Here we are on a hill that is supposed to be held by the enemy and not a shot fired, two hand grenades thrown by one scared A Scout. On the other hills, they are battling like wild cats. Mighty strange! Mighty strange! At that moment, Sam joined me beside the house. He said to me, "It looks as if we got this hill for nothing; I don't like it." I replied, "Well, we'll just sit still until the lieutenant gets here. There is just that one farmhouse left and no entrenchments, so if anyone is up there, they will have to be in that house. If they are, it doesn't make any difference because the rest of the squad is in the position to tear it down, and the balance of our platoon plus a machine-gun section is coming up the drawl."

Sam and I moved up to the row of hedges about ten yards from the house. From here, we could get a good view of the house and also the hills to the right and left without exposing ourselves. Just in front of the row of hedges, about five yards from the house, the side of the bank was dug out like one might see in a stone quarry. We lay behind the hedges, waiting for the lieutenant to come forward to give us the next move. Suddenly, Sam cried, "Look, the lieutenant and the rest of the platoon are coming up over to the left and exposing themselves on the crest of the hill."

We were not the only ones who had noticed this; for suddenly, the piercing, fearful sound of a sniper's rifle filled the air, and I heard someone yell, "Oh, God, I am hit."

The single shot from the sniper's rifle seemed to be a signal; for immediately, the rapid report of enemy machine guns were heard, and the bullets sang over our heads. I heard someone yell that our lieutenant had been hit by machine-gun fire. Sam and I opened fire on the house as telltale smoke had informed us that this is where the sniper was hidden. Our machine-gun section also opened fire on the house, and the sniper was soon silenced, but that didn't help the situation anyway. Two of the Jerries' machine guns still had everyone pinned to the earth, and no one could tell where they were located. We knew that the guns were not on the same hill as we were. If they had been American guns, we would have spotted them in a minute; for when the American machine gun is fired, it gives off smoke like a steel mill in Pittsburgh and belches fire like the dragons in the days of the knights of old. Any grandma, who was ninety years old, could pick up our guns, but not the enemy. They used powder that was smokeless and a flash hider that was superb. They fired from caves that were dug from the hillside. It was like trying to find four-leaf clovers.

Someone called back to the command post on the walkie-talkie and asked them if they could spot the point from where the enemy's fire was coming. They answered that they did not know the exact position of the guns, but the fire was coming from the hill to our left. Our next request was for 81-mm mortar fire on the hill.

The answer was, "The 81-mm mortars are now supporting troops in more desperate situations, and such support is limited because the pack mules have not completed the extremely hazardous trip up the mountain. Therefore, a shortage of ammunition exists."

Our response to them: "Well, please call to the rear and get some heavy artillery fire."

They to us, "Sorry, our quota for heavy rounds of artillery have been used up for today."

Did you hear that? "Our quota for heavy rounds of artillery have been used up for today." Maybe, we should just sit here and wait until tomorrow comes, and then we can have three more rounds like what they threw for us this morning. Boy, what a life! If those folks back home could only see us now. We were like clay pigeons on a shooting range. All those big guns to protect us, and they don't have any shells for today. This is like having a house on fire, a grand fire department, but no water. I imagine the firemen would throw sand. Well, this is just what we started doing, throwing sand, not at the enemy but out of a hole so that we could get in it. The order had come down to dig in and hold your positions. You think moles can dig; well, brother, you should see what soldiers produce when those tiny pellets called bullets fill the air.

Although we were expecting anything to happen, the chain of events, with their sudden upheaval, left us with the next move undecided; and for a moment, I forgot that some of our men had been killed and wounded by this destruction, which appeared suddenly like a shooting star, bursting into and across the heavens. A pleading voice and a staggering form soon placed me in the reality of things. It was the oldest man in the unit, and we nicknamed him Senior Soldier. He came staggering across the hill yelling, "I am hit, please, someone help me!" Only God knows why his legs were not cut from under him. He fell down beside Sam and me, who were crouched close to the quarrylike edge. Senior Soldier was the first man who had been hit. You know the one the sniper had picked. The downward flight of the bullet, through his body, clearly showed that the gun was fired from a high position, such as from a window in the house. I looked at Senior Soldier, lying there on his back. He was breathing rapidly, but with grunting difficulty, and his face was covered with water and salt from his sweat glands. In front of his neck, on the left side, was a small hole about the size of holes you see in loose-leaf notebook paper. The surrounding flesh looked as if it had been stretched larger than this small hole and then attempted to return to its normal position. The entire scene demonstrated the body's wonderful ability to compensate and to adjust to sudden emergency. Have you ever seen a puncture in a rubber ball after a sharp ice pick has been plunged into it and then removed? Did you notice how the rubber squeezes together to eliminate the puncture? So it appeared that nature had done the same for the hole in Senior Soldier's neck, and so well that externally, no blood flowed. I removed my first-aid packet, containing a small envelop of sulfanilamide powder. I poured it into the wound. Then I reached down and moved Senior Soldier's arm, which was in an awkward position. As I did, he cried out, "Oh, my back." I could see shivers of pain travel through his body like ocean waves, gliding across the sea. Sam and I raised him to a sitting position to take the pressure from his back. A large portion of his shirt was soaked with blood. We tore the shirt away from his body to expose his aching back. The bullet had entered his neck, traveling slightly downward and burst from his back in the area of the shoulder blade. It made just a small hole going in, but coming out, it took a plug out of his back about the size of the bottom of a quart-milk bottle. What was left had the appearance of soft, flabby flesh of a dark red color, and it moved up and down with Senior Soldier's breathing. A slow trickle of blood came from the wound. It dashed into the fibers of his woolen shirt with a seemingly gleeful escape. Then it spread itself out in all directions, like a drop of ink does when it falls upon a blotter. Sam and I knelt there in amazement. We were dumbfounded to see the ripping and tearing that a small bullet can do to a man's soft body. We shuddered to think that this could have been one of our bodies instead of Senior Soldier. Strange as it may seem, do you know what puts even more fear into our souls? We realized one thing; we must help this man. He is our brother and our responsibility. We must dress his wound. Stop the flow of blood from his body, lest he die at our feet and cause our conscience and dreams to haunt us eternally as though we ourselves had killed him with our helplessness. *God, don't let him die. Help us to think. Give us the courage to aid him.* I reached for my sulfanilamide powder. I poured it into the wound, hoping it would clog the wound as dirt does water. Then Sam poured his powder into the wound, and I quickly opened the bandage in my first-aid packet and pressed it against the wound. We had a problem. The wrapping attached to the bandage was not long enough to reach around his body to be tied. Two safety pins came from someplace, from some logical place, but I can't remember why they were carried or who carried them. I pinned one side of the bandage to Senior Soldier's torn shirt and then reached to pin the bandage on the other side of the torn shirt when, suddenly, we heard the split-second warning of a mortar shell as it scrapes through the air just before striking the earth.

The explosion dulled our ears. Dust, dirt, stones, and hot fragments flew in all directions. The shell landed about five yards from us. I wondered if I had been hit. I tried to see if I could feel any pain throughout my body. No, I felt all right. A little shaky, but nothing hurts. I looked around me. Sam was huddled in a small shelter that seemed to be dug out of the bank. He was okay. Senior Soldier was lying on his stomach, but no new wounds. I was lying on my stomach beside Senior Soldier, and do you know I was holding the bandage against his wound? I looked at my hand for a moment, wondering if it were mine. I didn't think about holding my hand against that bandage, but yet it was there. Can I say that I intended to do this for Senior Soldier? Nothing in my conscious mind informed me of what I was doing. I can't remember thinking to myself that I must press this bandage to his aching back. Sam couldn't recall how he got where he was and poor Senior Soldier cried out in despair, "We will never make it." A shell falling so close we thought should have killed us all. I raised up to a kneeling position over him and pinned the other side of the bandage to his torn shirt. Again, that fearful sound and the soul-shaking tone of an exploding shell. I didn't bother to stretch out this time. I just bent over in a crouched position across his back. I straightened up again and then, *Wham! Wham! Wham! Wham!*

Wham! Five shells fell in rapid succession. They all fell so close. None of them seemed over ten yards away, and all sort of substances flew about us in mad confusion.

My movements and reactions to this flurry of deadly missiles were the result of reflex reactions modified by a sort of confused thinking. The reflex action caused me to bend down across Senior Soldier's back to duck the flying pieces of steel. My confused thinking caused me to come back to a kneeling position after each shell had fallen, rather than remain in the logical bent position until all the shells had fallen. I found myself going up and down after each shell like a jack-in-the-box. After the fifth shell, I looked over at Sam who was still huddled in the dug-out bank, and I said to him, "Let's carry Senior Soldier out of here." Before I could offer any help to the wounded man, he was up on his feet and walking rapidly down the slope of the mountain. I nodded to Sam, "Let's go," and Sam began to tip lightly toward me as though he was walking on pins. He looked dazed and confused. As we walked, two shells fell nearby. We didn't bother to duck. We just kept walking as if we were already dead and could not be harmed. We even saw sparks fly from the granite rocks before us as air-splitting pieces of metal bounded off them. Yet Sam and I kept walking, and we didn't get a scratch. Now we were away from the immediate zone where the shells were falling and thinking once again in a sane manner, and we reverted to the snakelike tactics of crawling upon our stomachs. Not very far in front of us, we saw Senior Soldier, lying on his back, and seemed to be in great pain. He was having great difficulty breathing. Sam and I decided that Sam should stay here with him while I went to the bottom of the hill to see if I could locate some stretcher bearers. I started down the hill, half crawling, half rolling, and sometimes almost rising to a walking position. There it was again. The haunting sound of machine guns and that peculiar whine of bullets, looking for some soft muscles and organs in which to make a nest or a hard skull to crack and to push from it the brains and life of some human being who knew not what he would gain for risking so much but realized fully that he might lose his existence upon this earth. If he won this fight, would he experience a greater freedom and happiness in life than if he lost the fight? He had been told that the rewards for winning would be great, and that if he lost, he would be enslaved. Oh! What strange thoughts must have existed in the minds of many when they realized that before the fight, they enjoyed no such freedom and happiness, and that win or lose, there would be no such happiness and freedom. Will there be such happiness and freedom, or will we win or lose, be enslaved? Maybe, it is a battle for the lesser of two evils. Maybe, the leaders of our country are sincere, and there will be the freedom and happiness that is so-often spoken of. Certainly, not for a select group, but for all people. Perhaps, we had better win this fight and then see if we can gain that position that we so much desire. Dreaming and wondering again. This is certainly not the place or the time for it. Remember, there is a man lying there with a hole in his back as big as my fist. I have to do something about it.

I continued rolling and sliding down the hill until I had reached the bottom. Now it was safe for me to forget about enemy bullets for a moment. About a hundred yards in front of me, I spied the pleasing red cross on a white band that was pinned around the arm of a soldier. There were three of them, and one carried a folded stretcher on his shoulder. Usually, there were four men to a stretcher because of the rough mountainside over which they must travel with their suffering burdens. I trotted over to where they were and told them that we needed the stretcher to bring a wounded man down from the hills. I asked what had happened to the fourth man, and they informed me that he had stopped to help a man with a slight wound. One of the Red Cross men said they had received a call for a stretcher in this area, but they had been unable to locate the wounded man. I said, "Well, gentlemen, I don't know if I have the man you are looking for, but he definitely needs a stretcher." They said, "Okay, lead us to him."

We had just reached the drawl that would take us back up the hill when to our surprise who should burst through the bushes but Senior Soldier. He was staggering and stumbling like a drunken man. His clothing was dirty and disarranged. His dark beard showed well upon his almost-white skin. His long hair was spread about his head in a twisted manner. I reached for him with a supporting arm, lest he fall upon his face. We gently laid him on the stretcher with his eyes, gazing at the gray sky. To let him lie on his stomach would interfere too much with his breathing and cause great damage to his injured arm and collarbone. The first-aid men asked me to be the fourth stretcher bearer until they had reached the other first-aid man. We started across the small valley and back up that hill that we had come down before we reached the hill on which Senior Soldier had been wounded. As we puffed and pushed ourselves up the mountainside, I thought here is Senior Soldier—an American soldier. His body was reeking with pain. If you stood him in line with a platoon of white American soldiers, you would think that he too was what in American society is called a white man. His complexion was very light, and when he talked, there was no such dialect uttered from his lips as so many Americans like to pretend is always a part of any person who is classified as a Negro. Yes, here is Senior Soldier. He's a gentleman. He's brave. He has been fighting for his country. Now he has a big hole in him. Gee! I wish his whole big fertile country could see him now. God grant that he lives to return to his native land truly a valued citizen. Boy! That sort of thinking and reminiscing really helps.

We were almost halfway up the hill. Over on the hill, from which we had just come, I could see shells bursting and hear coming from these hills the sound of battle. For a moment, I was glad that I was helping to carry this stretcher. It offered the opportunity to remove the pressure and give me a chance to think. I fully realized that I must come back and join my platoon in whatever situation they existed. We were now at the top of the mountain. Down in the valley, below us, we could see the first-aid station. A doctor would be here who could really do something for Senior Soldier. There would be plenty of bandages, drugs, and blood plasma. The rest of the trip to the first-aid station would be downhill. This required much skill and balance on this tricky terrain, but it certainly would not be as bad as climbing uphill. Now we were almost to the house. The path resembled one leading to an anthill. Other stretcher bearers were coming in with their suffering cargoes from other units; and at the same time, other first-aid men were leaving the house with wounded men on stretchers, who had already received emergency treatment and would now be carried about three hard long miles down the mountainside to waiting ambulances and then driven miles and miles to operating tables. The trip alone was enough to kill any man.

At last, we were entering the door of the first-aid station. Immediately, another first-aid man met us and pointed out the place he wanted us to put the stretcher, bearing Senior Soldier. This first-aid man walked into the next room to call the doctor who was working on other men. The doctor came immediately. He took one look at Senior Soldier and called to one of his first-aid men to bring plasma. The doctor removed the rough bandage that I had applied. Quickly, the doctor applied medication to the wounds and then began to pack the large hole in Senior Soldier's back with gauze. Over this, he placed a bandage and taped it into place. I saw the first-aid man hang an inverted jar into the air. This jar had a small rubber hose with a needle on the end. The doctor stuck the needle into Senior Soldier's arm and taped it into place. Then the life water began to flow from the bottle into Senior Soldier's body at a slow and peaceful tempo. Now I felt better. Our suffering buddy was under a doctor's care. I glanced around the room. Several bottles hung in the air like canary birdcages on their stands and from each a small hose led down to a suffering form on a stretcher. These men were receiving plasma just as our buddy was. Here and there were other men whose wounds were not as serious.

One case in particular interested me. Here was a man who had been pinned down by machine-gun fire. One bullet had cut into his cartridge belt somewhere in the middle of his back. It was traveling parallel to the line of his body and straight up the middle of his back; it had made what appeared to be a superficial burn as though it meant not to harm the soldier, but merely to show to the world where the exact line should be drawn to divide him into two symmetrical halves. I thought, *Well, I guess I had better get back to my platoon.*

But then, the doctor called me over to where he was standing and said, "The fellow you just brought in will have to be carried down the mountain to an ambulance. We are short of stretcher bearers, so we will need you to help. Just wait around until the plasma has had a chance to work, and then I will call you."

I said, "Okay," and strolled out into the yard to escape from these examples of what could have been me or what still could happen to me.

The air was relaxing outside. The grass was still fresh green although it was near Thanksgiving Day. In front of the house, I spied a barn. Inside, I could see an assortment of arms and ammunition. Immediately, I arose and walked inside the barn to satisfy my curiosity. Here were M1s, carbines, pistols, knives, binoculars, cartridge belts, canteens, hand grenades, and many other pieces of equipment that fighting men carried. All of this had been left by the wounded and dying that had been brought to the first-aid station. Well, now I can stack up on arms and ammunition. Over in one corner, I spied a carbine. *Um-mm, let's see; I'll just take this carbine and leave my M1.* The carbine is a much-lighter weapon than the M1, and with it, I can move much faster. Furthermore, this carrying of M1-ammunition rounds in your cartridge belt really tires you out. I can get several clips of carbine ammunition, stuff them into my back pocket, and have less loading of the weapon to be bothered with. The M1 rifle held a clip that contained seven rounds, and it was a rather clumsy movement to stuff the clips into the chamber of the gun. The carbine held a magazine of twenty rounds, and it was quite easy to push the magazine up into the belly of the weapon. I picked up the carbine and several magazines of ammunition. Also, I stuffed an extra box of bullets into my back pockets and the large pockets of my field jacket. In addition, I salvaged three hand grenades and put them in my extra canteen cover, two first-aid packets, a trench knife, and a couple of boxes of K rations to dine on. I looked about the whole area of the barn, at all the stuff, and wished that I had a mule to carry it all. Well, I certainly can't do it. So turning my back on this paraphernalia of death, I strolled out into the pathway leading to the house and sat on a big rock.

As I sat on the rock, I noticed something that was very strange. Soldiers who passed by hesitated and peered at my face in a peculiar manner. They looked at me with disbelief as though I was a ghost. Finally, one spoke. Pointing his finger at me, he said, "Look at your helmet." I slowly removed the steelhead protector and rejected what I saw as unbelievable. Wedged in my helmet, slightly above the eye, was a steel fragment from an exploded mortar shell. The fragment was approximately two inches in length and about one-half inch wide. It struck with such force that it bent double, punching through the steel helmet, and remaining wedged like a woodpecker in its nest. The metal outer helmet does not rest on your head but contains a separate, plastic-inner coat that fits snugly inside the steel helmet. The separate, plastic-inner coat can also be worn as a head covering. The plastic covering does not rest directly on one's head but is suspended on a network of leather bands shaped like a head that rest in contact with the human flesh of the head. The plastic-inner covering and/or the steel helmet are, shall we say, suspended over the head as protecting elements. You have sort of a fort hanging over your skull and brains. The miracle is the fact that the steel-mortar piece had punched holes in both the steel outer covering and in the inner-plastic covering, stopping about a quarter inch from the leather band that rested on my forehead. It seems like it was coming very close to brain damage or sudden death. It looked like a miracle to me. My own, personal miracle. I shall cling to this "steel through steel" as long as I can so that I can show to the world that miracles are real.

I must have sat there for an hour, listening to the rumbling of cannons, thinking of home, thinking of what we were involved in, and wondering how the fellows were making out. It was now afternoon, and it wouldn't be long before darkness would set in, for the days were very short during this time of the year. I certainly hope that we can get Senior Soldier down the hill before it gets dark. I don't want to be stumbling about in this unfamiliar territory at night. I sat here about ten minutes more just daydreaming until one of the aidmen called me and said that the doctor had given the order for Senior Soldier to be carried down the mountain. This time, there were only three of us. Two would carry the stretcher while the other led the way. I started out leading since I had a weapon. The other two men who were permanent first-aid men were not allowed to carry guns. The trip down the mountain was long and hard. It must have required about six hours. Four of these were during darkness, and much of the time was spent in resting, doubling back when we got off the trail and groping through the black night. We were constantly in fear that we might make the wrong turn and stumble into enemy lines or mines. Our greatest help was some telephone wires that we were able to follow as a guide. Senior Soldier suffered an awful lot the first hour of the trip, but then the morphine given to him by the doctor relieved him some. We walked for five hours before we ran across any American soldiers. The last hour was with much less anxiety since we had seen some of our troops and received directions. At the bottom of the mountain, we found the ambulance waiting. The driver and his assistant quickly checked Senior Soldier to see if the blankets were around him good; then we lifted him inside. Two other men were already inside on stretchers. The ambulance driver closed and tested his doors. The motor started up. The small parking lights were turned on. They were off. There goes Senior Soldier. Well, that's that. A hard long trip it was for him. Gee! I wish his whole big fertile country could have seen him.

"Well, fellows, we have to fight with these mountains again," I said. One of the medics looked at me and replied, "I wouldn't advise you to go clambering up that mountainside at this hour of the morning. You don't know the password, and you may just get shot by one of your own men. Why don't we find a nearby farmhouse and get some sleep. Then we can go up at daybreak." Frankly, this suggestion just suited me fine. As tired as my back and legs were and as shaky as my nerves had become, I couldn't help but be greedy for a chance to sleep in some place where I could close both eyes instead of only one. I thought I hope that the fellows don't think I have run out on them. The three of us soon located a small farmhouse. As I fell off to sleep with the hard top of a wooden bench, pushing up against my back, I just faintly remember my two medic companions and a middle-aged Italian couple before an open fireplace and engaged in a pleasant conversation with a conglomeration of Italian and English languages.

In the morning, I had a tasty breakfast of pork and eggs, hard crackers, coffee, and fruit bars, which were supplied by the medics. Before departing, the aidmen gave the Italian couple two boxes of K rations. The couple expressed their gratitude so strongly that one would have thought the stretcher bearers had given the Italian couple a herd of cattle.

The three of us started back up the mountain: one grim infantry scout with a carbine and two unarmed medics with a stretcher. On their arms was the red cross with the white background—the sign of the angels to a smitten soldier. On the way up the mountain, we passed a mule train loaded with food and ammunition for our men. Several of the paisons yelled and screamed at the mules to keep them moving. Below the path, about fifty yards down the side of the mountain, I saw two paisons dissecting one of the mules, which lay sprawled on the ground as though it had fallen down the hill. The paisons tried to tell us that the mule had fallen down the mountain and had broken a leg, so it had to be shot. The mule was then being cut up into small pieces so that later, it could be prepared in some fine-style dish for a meal. The medics informed me that the mules are sometimes pushed off the trail so that they can be eaten for food. Whether this story was true or started as a joke as so many things do, I could not say. On we plodded until we reached a path, leading to the aid station. Here, I said good-bye to the aidmen and thanked them. They bid me good luck, and I continued up the mountain in search of my company command post.

I found the command post located in a small straw hut in the area where I had slept under the raincoat in the early morning before we jumped off on our attack. The first individual I sighted was our captain. He was as neat and clean as a ninety-day wonder is when he first comes out of Officer Candidate School. His trousers were neatly creased; his boots were shined, and around his neck was a pretty blue scarf. The very sight of him inspired me. Yes, here he stood like a ray of golden sunshine, glowing through a vastness of dark clouds, like the evening star, shining in the heavens at night, like an oasis on a boundless desert. How did it affect his men when they saw him like this? To his men, it carried a message of faith, determination, and courage. The captain was beyond the shadow of a doubt greatly uplifting to the morale of the men merely by checking his personal appearance while under the stress and strain of battle. I braced myself, waiting for a barrage of strong language. Instead I got, "Hi, you, glad to see you back. Your platoon is dug in on the forward slope of this hill. Here is a pair of dry socks. See that you change into a dry pair every day." The rest of his words were of the kind that make you feel as though you have done a good job.

I said so long to the captain and began scuffling with the oozy stuff, which seemed always to be present upon the hills. As I plodded along, I ran into two soldiers who were leading another one down the mountain. I inquired, "What's wrong with him?"

One soldier replied, "I don't know; he seemed to just start acting irrationally."

We were sitting in our foxholes when, all of a sudden, he started yelling, "I'll kill 'em all." Then he jumped out of his foxhole and started running toward the enemy. After going about ten yards, he fell over a rock and ran into a tree. Several of the fellows grabbed him. He was as blind as a bat. He couldn't see his hand before his face. We looked at his eyes. They looked perfect. Not a scratch, nothing, I tell you. He just couldn't see. He was blind. Nothing else, just blind. I stood there looking as they led him to the aid station. I had seen the blank stare that only comes from eyes that do not see. And as I saw them disappear along the trail, I began to dream. Yes, dream in the daytime of what I had just seen. It all seemed so strange. Why does a man cease to see when no physical harm has come to his eyes? Why does a man suddenly think that he can destroy an army? Are there not things other than bullets or shells that can destroy man? Did he want to fight? Why did he want to kill? Who did he want to kill? Was it the enemy before him, or was it the fact that all his life he had been denied the dignity of living? Was it the fact that all his life, he had been pushed aside, prevented from entering because he was Black? Denied education because he was Black? Denied jobs because he was Black? Fired because he was Black? Kept from voting because he was Black? Laughed at because he was Black? Made fun of by jokes in movies, on stages? Scorned, spit at, cursed at, and blamed for all things that went wrong? Can you see two thoughts in his mind? The first thought: fight for freedom; kill those who would enslave the world; fight for democracy. The second thought: you are already enslaved; you are the scum of the earth; you are a segregated soldier; you are no good and that is why we separate you. I ask, can you see these two thoughts, both fighting to be foremost until they had destroyed this man's ability to see anything? I ask you, who did he wish to kill when he ran from his foxhole, a sightless mass of confusion? Did he want to kill the enemy in the first thought, or did he want to kill the second thought? He said, "I'll kill 'em all." Maybe he meant both thoughts. You tell me my big fertile country;

you tell me. My daydreaming ended when my drifting eyes came to rest upon a blanket, lying upon the ground, evidently belonging to no one. I gathered the blanket into my arms as I would certainly need it if I slept in these hills tonight.

I resumed my journey upon the muddy slopes and over the crest of the hill, and on the forward slope, I found my platoon resting in shallow foxholes that were body long in length so that one could stretch out and sleep. In the first foxhole, I came upon the sergeant. He was in charge now because our second lieutenant had been killed by machine-gun fire almost immediately after Senior Soldier had been shot by the sniper. The sergeant said, "Hi, Nat, the medics sent word that you were taking Senior Soldier down the mountain. I didn't know if you would be back or not."

I replied, "Yep, I'm back, but I'm not bragging about it." The sergeant replied, "I guess you wonder how we got on this hill and what happened. Well, after you left with Senior Soldier, we received orders to sit tight on the other hill until dark and in the morning withdraw at the signal. We lost five men from machine-gun fire, but the other platoons were pretty well shot up and had to withdraw immediately. The other companies were in even worse difficulty than us. The enemy is well dug in, and you can't go running up these hills, trying to poke at them with sticks; first, you need a big artillery strike to rock these hills. The fellows are bitter because they couldn't get artillery support. Anyhow, we were the last platoon to pull back. We stayed on the hill until darkness, and then we quietly withdrew to this hill. Frankly, I wish we had stayed on the other hill. If the enemy ever found out that we were on the forward slope of this hill, they could point their 88mms right in our foxholes." I said to the sergeant, "Where is Sam?"

The sergeant replied, "They sent him back to the rear; a shell fell close to him. No fragments hit him, but he had a wrenched back." I stood silent for a while until the sergeant said, "There is an empty foxhole over there. You had better get in it, and don't do any moving around unless you want to bring shell fire on your head. We'll decide later who is to sleep and who is to stand guard tonight."

I said, "Okay," and left. As I moved across the area, the fellows spoke softly and bid me welcome back into the fold. I jumped into an empty foxhole and spread my blanket upon the ground. Just as I was about to relax in popped our comrade, we nicknamed Private First Class. I asked, "How is everything in your hometown?"

Private First Class said, "Everything is okay according to the last letter I received. The reason I came over is because you own the only blanket on the hill, and knowing what a kind heart you have and also realizing how cold these nights can get, I know you won't mind my sharing the night with you and your blanket."

I said, "You know, Private First Class, I had just finished thinking how nice it would be to roll up in this blanket, and here you come. Okay, stay in, and I'll let you sit up all night and do guard duty."

Private First Class and I talked until sundown about old times, about going home, and about what happened the day before. The night guard duty assignments were made, and the password was sent around. Private First Class and I rolled up in our blanket and dozed off. We didn't sleep much. The cold and dampness kept us shivering. To make matters worse, there was a continued tug-of-war over the blanket. About three o'clock in the morning, I was fed up. I tapped Private First Class on the shoulder and said, "Do you mind returning to your own foxhole?"

Private First Class looked at me like a cocker spaniel does and said, "Gee, if I leave, you'll be colder than you are now. Look, I was in a foxhole with Snags before, and he snores."

I said, "Oh, he does; well, it sounds mighty peaceful over there now." I should not have said that for I heard the still-night air pierced by a sound that reminded me of twenty rattlesnakes doing a shake dance. "Doggone," I muttered, "everybody in Italy must know where we are."

We started tossing stones into Snags's hole to wake him up. A couple of stones found their mark and Snags woke up yelling, "What's up? What's up?" Private First Class said, "Nothing, you dope; you were snoring again."

"What time is it," whispered Snags.

"Three," Private First Class replied.

"Thanks for waking me up; it is time for me to go on guard duty," Snags replied.

Good old Snags. Before Snags came over seas, the army pulled out his two front teeth. When he asked about replacements, they told him, "You are going to fight 'em, not bite 'em. Snags wasn't biting them, but he sure was snoring at them." Private First Class plopped down in the foxhole and got under his half of the blanket, and I did the same. The next morning, we were eating breakfast when two rounds of our 60-mm mortar shells fell on a house across on the next hill. To our surprise, nine or ten enemy troops came running out of the house. One of our water-cooled machine guns opened up and began cutting the poor devils down. Some ran back into the house. Two more mortar shells struck the house, and about fifty enemy troops swarmed out of the house. They never had a chance. The water cool, and the mortar shells cut them down. The fellows opened up with their M1s. It isn't often you catch the enemy out of their shelter like this. It was all over in fifteen minutes. Only two or three of the enemy managed to escape over the top of the hill.

All was peaceful and quiet again. Then way back in the enemy territory, I heard a low *loom a loom* and then the whining ever-increasing sound of an 88mm shell, bearing down upon us and then skimming over our heads and exploding in the valley behind us. Again, *loom a loom,* and this shell fell in the valley in front of us. One in front and one behind. They were zeroing in on us. The next one would be right in there. *Loom a loom. Wham!* Dust and steel flew. *Loom a loom. Wham!* Each one sounded as though it was falling in your hole. All day, this went on. One shell about every ten minutes until five shells had fallen, then a half-hour break. Some went over our heads, and some fell in the valley below. When they fell in the valley below, we could hear the hot steel whirring through the air and striking tree limbs until it had spent itself. One shell landed in a hole that had two soldiers in it. The fragments killed one of them immediately; the other was shielded by the first one's body and didn't get a scratch. I saw the dead soldier's body carried across the forward slope to the reverse side of the hill.

When night came, I was glad to see it. The enemy artillery ceased to fall, and our nerves were relaxed. The next day, things were still peaceful and calm. We stayed in our foxholes, not daring to come out for fear of drawing fire. In the evening, before it became dark, four soldiers in single file came strolling across our area, carrying rations for another company. This brought more enemy fire upon our heads. When the shells had ceased, I peeped from my hole to see if everything was okay. Arising from one of the foxholes, I saw a small wisp of smoke slowly curling upward into space. All eyes from all foxholes were upon this slow bluish wisp of smoke that glided from the hole in an evil-sneering manner. Several men called out, "Are you okay?" No answer, just peaceful quiet. Snags was the first to reach his foxhole. A call was sent to the medic. It was no use; a shell had fallen in one of our comrade's foxhole. A direct hit. Another man was gone. We had killed some enemies. We had lost some buddies. Someone will say you killed fifty to two. What difference does this make? It doesn't make up for your buddies. It only means that fifty-two men are dead. We didn't bother our comrade's body. We just left it in his foxhole. That night, we gathered around and buried him in his foxhole. Someone said a prayer, and then we stuck a stick in the ground and put his helmet on it, so his body could be found and taken to a military cemetery.

The next day, we left this hill and moved to a more forward and higher position held by another company. I spied about thirty men. The rest of them would join us tomorrow, and then the two companies, which usually totaled about four hundred men, would attack the next mountain. Always the next mountain. Rations and ammunition were brought up to us and also packs containing our pup tents and blankets. Private First Class and I picked out a foxhole that had already been dug, which was located in the very center of the middle of the hill, which was shaped like a perfect horseshoe. It started raining before we were in position good. We tried to rig up our pup tent across the top of the hole so as to keep out the water, but it always found some way to get in and make life miserable.

The whole night was rough. One man had to stay awake in each foxhole. Private First Class and I spent the night taking turns at watch, sleeping three hours and then watching three hours. Once in a while, the enemy would slip up to the top of the hill and roll hand grenades down. You would hear the grenade rolling down the hill then duck and hope that it exploded before it got to your foxhole. Private First Class and I made a decision that if one rolled into our hole, we would not try to get out but would take a chance on trying to throw the grenade out.

When day came, I was glad to see it. Sometimes, you wish for nightfall. Other times, you wish for daylight. With daylight came the rest of the other company with whom we were to attack the next hill. Fifteen muddy, unshaven soldiers appeared. "Is this Company L?" I asked.

"Yep, this is it," answered the sergeant from Company L.

Our sergeant said, "Where are the rest of your men?"

The sergeant from Company L responded, "Well, can you see that big mountain over there? Some of them were killed there. Do you see the valley way in the distance to our rear? Well, some of them are in the hospital back there. Do you know where the aid station is? Some of them are there with trench foot and pneumonia." Company L has fifty men altogether, and there should be two hundred. Company I has one hundred men, and there should be two hundred.

"Say, Sergeant, what about the attack?" I asked.

The sergeant said, "It has been called off. We are supposed to just stay here and hold this ground."

I turned from the sergeant and said to one of the soldiers from Company L, "Look here, Soldier, why can't you get some replacements in your company?" He said. "Look, bud, they don't train Colored soldiers to fight; they train them to load ships, and you don't expect them to put white boys in a Negro outfit, do you? What do you think this is a democracy or something?" That last crack got me. It took the wind out of my sails; my car was out of gas again. I looked around; the other fellows had caught the remark also. One minute, our morale is up; the next minute, it's down. I snatched up my carbine and started to my foxhole to tell Private First Class the news. As I walked, I muttered to myself, *I wish I was loading a boat.*

When I reached the foxhole, Private First Class wasn't there. I asked a soldier nearby if he had seen Private First Class, and he said that he had gone over to another foxhole, which had several fellows in it. Boy, I was burning. Private First Cass had come to my foxhole when I had the only blanket, and now that he had found a better place, he was gone again. I sat in my foxhole, wet, soaked, and chilled to the bone. If only this blasted rain would cease.

For the next couple of hours, the only comfort I received was from singing "Ink Spots'" songs and reciting the Twenty-third Psalm over and over again. When I got to the part, "Yea, though I walk through the valley of the shadow of death, I will fear no evil, for thou art with me," waves of courage would leap through my veins. The only reason I had survived, the only reason I was composed was I believed there was a God, and that this God would not let me die upon these hills. No amount of guns, no amount of men, no belief in democracy or anything else was capable of giving to me the security, protection, and courage that I needed in order to survive physically and mentally. The only thing was my faith in God. Even though I was part of an army with numerous superiors over me, I am still an individual; and when involved with life and death struggles, some self-preserving decision must be made. I decided that it was time to get rid of these wet, cold clothes that were upon my back. I left my hole and went down the mountainside to the aid station. Once inside, I received a royal welcome from the medics. They gave me a blanket to wrap up in while my clothes dried in front of a hot fire. They gave me hot soup and canned beans and franks as well.

After my clothes dried, I felt like a new man. I took up my carbine and started back to my foxhole. The first foxhole I spotted when I reached the area was the one Private First Class had moved to. It did look rather comfortable. It was dug out in the side of the mountain, and the pup tent flaps were draped across the front. This was an efficient arrangement for keeping out the rain. I walked over and pulled back the flap. There sat Private First Class with three other fellows having a wonderful time, shooting the breeze. I said, "Look here, Private First Class, if you don't come out of there and get in that other foxhole, I'll go down to the aid station and get a casualty tag."

Private First Class seemed quite amused at this statement. He said, "Okay, let's go back to your mudhole." We spent several more days on this hill, ducking hand grenades and watching for the enemy to attack. It rained almost every day, and the fellows stayed wet. Trench foot took a heavy toll. On Thanksgiving Day, the army lived up to its promise, and we had turkey and dressing even with cranberries on the side.

One morning, Private First Class and I sat in our foxhole making coffee. We would put a part of the wax box that covered our rations in my steel helmet. We would put some powdered coffee and water in a canteen cup and add several lumps of sugar. Next, a match was put to the wax paper, and our canteen cup was set in the helmet, and the coffee was brewed. That was the worst coffee I have ever seen made; it contained burnt paper instead of cream. On the other hand, it was the best coffee I have ever tasted. To a cold, damp body, nothing could seem better than this hot, sweet stuff. Private First Class tossed back his head, his eyes to the sky, ready to take a sip. He said, "Ah, wonderful, soothing fluid, come to my waiting jaws." Then he froze with the canteen cup almost to his lips. He said, "Say, Nat, do you see what I see?" I looked up. The dark clouds were rolling aside like a curtain does for the first act of a bright musical show on Broadway. Blue sky was making a stage of splendor and, out upon the stage, danced gleeful sunbeams, singing their songs of joy. Curtain of dark clouds. A stage of blue sky. Little sunbeams as actors. Yes, that's the way it looks when you haven't seen the sun for almost fifteen days. We leapt from our muddy foxholes to let the sunshine upon us, and then I spied the most important part of the show. It was the audience; every man had come from his foxhole. Every eye had turned to the skies. Everyone of us was on Broadway. Everyone of us was seeing the show. Down in the valley, we heard a church bell toll. All eyes turned to the valley below. The fog and mist had cleared away. We could see a town and in it a little red church. Do you know we didn't even know the church was there? How sweetly the bells did sound. We thought we were so alone on our little-high horseshoe mountain when just below us, people were living; life was still going on and on. All eyes showed signs of daydreaming. All minds were aglow with sweet daydreams of the little church in their village. The little church in their countryside or the big church in their city. I said, "Private First Class, is today Sunday morning?"

He didn't look from the village, he just replied, "What other morning could start like this?" The sergeant broke up the peace and quiet with some wonderful news. He said, "Men, pack your junk; we will be leaving here about dusk. We are going back to the rear and reorganize."

The rest of the morning, I just lulled in the sun. In the afternoon, I packed my gear and cleaned the mud from my carbine. About dusk, we left our horseshoe mountain. As we crossed the area where our comrade had died, I glanced back at the stick still standing in the ground with his torn helmet, hanging from the top. As we walked down the trail, I said, "Sergeant, where are the men who were supposed to have taken over our position when we left."

He replied, "There aren't any. The line was set up about one thousand yards to our rear. I heard that we were not supposed to be launching an attack anyhow. That's why we didn't get artillery support. Someone in the rear decided they wanted to gamble a little bit, so they ran us up a few hills. Others say it is just part of the routine of keeping the enemy busy, so they won't ship any troops to Germany. The enemy is here to keep you from going to Germany, and you are here to keep them from going to Germany. So both of you go right on killing each other off and hoping your side wins in Germany." Getting down off the mountain was simple compared to getting up. The fellows were fresh and clean when they came here; but now, they were tired, muddy, and dirty; and most of them had grown haggard beards and needed haircuts. One could plainly see the discomfort that had been inflicted by foot trouble. Most of the men limped as though they had nails sticking through the bottom of their boots.

At the bottom of the mountain, a convoy of trucks was waiting. They whisked us far to the rear where we once again went through the procedure of taking baths. The arrangement for receiving clean clothes was very efficiently run. The shower unit was a large trailerlike truck that was enclosed. You would enter by a pair of steps into a small room where you were given a cloth bag. In this bag, you were told to put all of your clothes. On the bag were two identification numbers. After putting your clothes in the bag, you would give the bag to a waiting soldier and keep one of the numbers to claim clean clothes. Then you entered the shower, which was a long, narrow passageway that was the full length of the van. You had to pass along slowly, washing and moving like automobiles on an assembly line. There was a continuous stream of soldiers moving through this arrangement, which contained about twenty shower sprays within its entire length. When you stepped from the other end of this shower passageway, you were given a towel by a waiting soldier. After you had dried off, you presented your number to another soldier behind a counter who gave you in return a bag containing the exact number and kind of articles of clothing that you had put in the other bag, only these were fresh and clean. When the entire company had finished showering, we loaded on trucks and were taken to a bivouac area. Here we pitched our pup tents. Later, we ate a good, hot supper, and then a tired bunch of soldiers lay down to sleep away thoughts of horror.

CHAPTER FIVE

ON PASS

Our company remained in this safe bivouac area for a full week. Most of the time, we spent on pass in the town of Viareggio. Viareggio is a beautiful level town on the east coast of Italy, and to its left lies beautiful white sandy beaches that bound the Ligurian Sea. A friendly town it was with many small bars and numerous restaurants. My favorite pastime was to go to a small restaurant close to the water's edge and order a steak and french-fried potatoes. Viareggio is often spoken of as the Atlantic City of Italy, but the warmth and friendliness of Viareggio devoid of any desires for gain of money far surpasses anything Atlantic City has to offer.

When we left this rest haven, our company took up positions on the front in the flat-left coastal region rather than going again into the mountains. We were here strictly for defensive reasons. Our mission was to keep the enemy where he was. In the daytime, we hid in small houses along the front so as not to draw enemy-artillery fire. As soon as it became dark, we moved out into our foxholes and watched throughout the night to prevent enemy patrols from probing our lines. The nights were cold, dark, and a tester of nerves. The foxholes were twenty-five yards apart, but the area we covered was so great that we could only put two men in every other foxhole, leaving a gap of fifty yards for enemy movement. One man in the foxhole watched while the other man slept. All sorts of sounds could be heard as the blowing winds stirred the bushes and made them look like moving men. Small wonder it is that we welcomed the coming of dawn so that we could return to the comfort of our hiding places and enjoy the good vision of daylight. This move from our foxholes back to the house was always made just as day began to break and before it had become light enough for the enemy to see our movements.

One morning, just as I returned from a chilly night of peering into the darkness, my platoon leader looked at me and said, "Say, Nat, I hear you have a birthday coming up Christmas, how would you like to spend it in Rome?"

"In Rome," I replied.

"Boy, that would be great." The lieutenant said, "Okay, then get your things together and report to the first sergeant at the command post. Tell him you are the man going on pass from the third platoon."

I practically leapt for joy. On pass at a rest camp! In Rome for Christmas!

When I reached the command post, the company jeep was already there and waiting. The first sergeant knew I was coming and had my pass ready when I arrived. I hopped in the front seat of the jeep, and the driver, seeing that I was eager to get going, said, "We are waiting for TS."

"Good," I replied. "I'll have some company." TS as the driver had called him had the right name. He was the tallest soldier in the unit and we had nicknamed him TS. He was about six feet five inches tall, and I guess he weighed about 225 pounds. TS looked to me to be about thirty years old. He had a heavy mustache, a big face, and a heavy, booming voice. He sort of reminded me of the massive giant that used to appear when Aladdin rubbed his wonderful lamp. When we were back in the States, TS used to be in the drum and bugle corps. He was the guy who beat the gigantic bass drum and could he make some noise. Don't get me wrong now. TS wasn't the empty barrel type that makes a lot of noise. He was noted for his courage and liked by everyone. The noise was a part of him, but he was a good guy.

Strange thing, TS and I always seemed to pop up in the same places. Why, when our platoon was on the hill where Senior Soldier was shot, who did I run into but TS. Here I was going on pass and who was going but TS. I had sat in the jeep ten minutes, thinking about TS, when he walked up to the jeep and said, "Hi you doing, Nat? You going on pass too?"

I replied, "Yep, as soon as you load on this jeep."

TS leapt into the rear of the jeep and said, "Okay, let's roll." Roll we did. We were on our way to the regimental headquarters where we would take another jeep. Before you get there, you must pass an open stretch of roadway about two miles in length. The Jerries up in the mountains could see every vehicle that traveled this road. The driver knew this, for practically, every jeep driver in the 92nd Infantry Division had dodged 88mms on this road, and some of them didn't make it. The drivers had named this stretch Purple Heart Lane.

As we rounded the bend to hit Purple Heart Lane, the driver said, "Gentlemen, hold your helmets." With that, he shoved his foot to the floor. The little jeep almost shot from under us. The few bushes and piles of stones on our right and left seemed to be flying by us in the opposite direction. As the little car flashed down this roadway, I thought I might as well had stayed in my foxhole as to risk getting killed going eighty and ninety miles an hour in a jeep. I was much relieved when the driver eased his foot from the floor, and we rounded a slight curve in a manner that for many would have required the use of toilet tissue.

We were under the cover of stone houses and heavy foliage. TS breathed a sigh and said, "I think I would rather drive a little slower and let the Jerries shoot at me."

The driver said, "Pay it no mind. I go through this at least twice every day and three times on Sunday." Now, we were stopping at a large gate, which was the entrance to a spacious yard in the middle of which stood a massive house. This was regimental headquarters. We were greeted by a second lieutenant, and the first thing he did was tell us that it was not Rome we were going to but Florence, known in the Italian language as Firenze. Florence is a very old and famous city. It was known the world over for its large, ancient stone buildings and its historic bridges to say nothing of the fact that it at one time in history was the center of world culture.

Next, we climbed into another jeep, and we were taken to a place a half mile from regimental headquarters. Here, TS and I joined with other soldiers from the entire regiment who were going on pass. Waiting here also were two large convoy trucks that were to take us to Florence. A sergeant met us and showed us to a portable kitchen where we ate a big meal. After eating, we climbed aboard the truck and made a pleasant journey across the yet green countryside of beautiful Italy. The distance we covered was close to fifty-five miles before we entered the city of Florence.

As soon as we had crossed the city limits, one could sense the spirit of Christmas in the air. Troops in almost every unit of the Fifth Army were in town, and you could see the glow of anticipated Christmas Day joy radiating from their faces. All shoes sparkled like diamonds; and the scarfs of color, to tell the type of outfit, stood out brightly against the dull olive drab so as to make each soldier seem a bright and lively creature.

Men from the infantry wore a clear blue; those from the artillery wore a fiery red; those from the cavalry wore a golden yellow; and from all types of other units were scarfs of color. Over their chests were ribbons of honor, Good Conduct ribbons, Bronze Star ribbons, Silver Star ribbons, Combat Infantryman badges, campaign ribbons with battle stars, oak-leaf clusters; and if we had looked hard enough, we might have seen ribbons for Distinguished Service Crosses, and even a Medal of Honor. On the left shoulder of each soldier was a patch of small cloth, which was the sign of his division or outfit. Those from the tank destroyers wore the glowing tiger head; those from the Thirty-fourth Division wore the skull of a steer, and many others were about too numerous to mention. Every GI had his trousers creased sharp enough to cut fine silk, and each one looked like a schoolboy, playing hockey on the first warm day of spring. Many GIs had upon their arms, pretty, smiling girls, those gentle beings, that make the world go round. Among all of this moved the citizens of this land, men, women, boys, and girls. A glorious sight this was to this truckload of soldiers as we glanced around the streets. Why, we could see every mixture of races of mankind at a single glance. Many strange nationalities from the British Eighth Army added more color. We began to straighten our ties and check our shoes. We glanced at our ribbons of honor and proudly held up our left shoulders that carried the patch with the American buffalo, which said that we were from the 92nd Infantry Division. We knew that we were, at this moment, part of the picture before us whose splendor was so exaggerated by the trying conditions that we had just left.

The truck on which we were riding was now entering a large square, and facing the square was a massive structure. This was the rest camp. It reminded me of the Union Station in Washington, D.C., where you go to catch a train. As soon as we stepped through the door, we went to a booth, which had a large sign saying, Registration. We were greeted by a Wac in the booth who said, "Welcome, fellows, to the city of Florence Rest Haven. How would you like to be our guests for the next three days?" Beaming faces gave an answer better than any word.

TS said, "This is what I have been waiting for." After we had registered, we were given a book of meal tickets to cover this night's meal and meals for the next three days. We were also assigned sleeping quarters. The last thing the Wac said was, "Gentlemen, the city is yours."

First, we went to our sleeping quarters and deposited our extra clothing. On the way there we had to go outside of the great hall in which we had registered, and here we saw railroad tracks and a loading platform, which confirmed our belief that this had once been a railroad station. We washed up while we were in our quarters, and then each one set out on his way to explore the place. Was it fine! A large ballroom floor with an orchestra. Spacious game rooms with ping-pong tables, card tables, checkers, chess, and pool tables. A well-stacked reading room and library. A lounge with soft chairs. A theater. A music room where those who wanted to play the piano could do so. Small store counters where you could purchase almost anything. The dining room was magnificent. Chandeliers hung from the ceiling; the chairs were of antique mahogany, and the tables, large enough for four, were covered with white linen. To top all of this, you ate on china plates and with real knives and forks. Dessert too! Can you imagine that?

After supper, I went to the rest-camp movie. Then for an hour, I listened to a GI playing the piano in the music room.

All of this I did alone, enjoying some pleasant moments of solitude. Most of them centered about how fortunate I was. When I retired that night, I really slept well.

The next morning, which was Christmas Eve and my birthday, I slept so long that when I did arise, it was too late for breakfast. Lunch was being served. This was one fine day for me. At lunch, I met an old friend from army days in the States. By night, we had thoroughly explored the town of Florence, eaten a hearty Christmas Eve dinner, taken in a movie, played six games of ping-pong, three hands of pinochle, and gone to a dance. It was well after two o'clock when we both retired, and Christmas was already with us.

Despite the fact that I had gone to bed late, the next morning, I was up by nine thirty. The reason for my haste was a religious Christmas service that was being conducted at the rest camp by an army chaplain. When I arrived for the service, the room was already filled, and I had to stand. At lunch time, I joined three soldiers, and we four poked about the town talking and mingling with the holiday crowd. It was close to supper time when we returned to the rest center.

I ran into TS on the way to supper, and we decided to eat together. Much to our surprise, a long line had formed leading to the dining room. There must have been twenty soldiers trying to join the line at once, which created a sort of jockeying for position. I heard TS, and a white soldier exchange some stern words. The white soldier's face twisted in rage, and he cried out loudly, "You Black son of a—." You could have heard a pin drop after his words echoed through the lobby. Both TS and the white soldier sensed each other's next move. Like tap dancers doing an act, each sprung away from the other, and each reached for a concealed trench knife. TS reached inside his belt, and the white soldier reached at the area of his hip pocket. I grabbed TS's arm. I knew I couldn't hold him if he wanted to go.

I yelled, "TS, let him go; he doesn't know what he's saying." Four other white soldiers grabbed the soldier and were hauling him away. Meanwhile, TS snatched his arm away from me.

He looked down and said, "That's all you guys ever say is; let him go." Then TS looked about so as to catch every eye in the line, and he yelled out in his booming voice, "The next guy who calls me anything other than my name will get his guts cut out."

TS was throwing a challenge. He had just about said, "I wish someone would say something to me." No one accepted his challenge. They all seemed to look at him in the same way. Their eyes all said, we don't blame you fellow. You have a right to blow your top. We are as sorry as you that this happened, but don't blame us. You were right, and the other guy was wrong. TS pulled himself together, and we both got back in line. TS turned to me and said, "I didn't mean to yell at you, but that guy made me mad."

I said, "Yep, I know. Can't blame you. It only takes one soldier like that to set off a powder keg. Most of these guys in the line are pretty decent fellows."

TS said, "I hope you are right." When TS and I reached a table and got our food, the turkey and dressing were so delicious that we soon forgot about the disturbing incident. After supper, we attended a Christmas program that included the singing of Christmas carols and, of course, the traditional Christmas play with "Tiny Tim." The last event for the night was a dance. When I left to hit the sack well after Christmas had passed, TS was still enjoying the song and dance.

The next day at nine in the morning, we loaded on our trucks, got into our company jeep, and headed back to regimental headquarters. Once again, a mad dash along Purple Heart Lane. Then I was back on the front. You can bet I spent the rest of the day telling the fellows in the platoon about the three fabulous days that I had spent in Florence.

Our company remained at the immediate front for only two days after I came back from Florence, and we were relieved by another outfit. We moved not off the front, but just slightly to the rear. We were now the battalion in reserve for any emergency. We could move around and breathe easily, but we kept our guns in position and stayed on the alert.

CHAPTER SIX

BIG PATROL

Our platoon was enjoying the peace and quiet of being in reserve. It was only necessary to post about six men on watch during the night, so we slept well and got plenty of rest. Meanwhile, two patrols had been sent out by troops in the coastal region to capture prisoners because, for some reason, the brass in the rear was in urgent need of information. Neither of these patrols had returned with any prisoners. The brass becoming disturbed with this, decided to send out three night patrols of full companies each to capture prisoners. It so happened that our company was one of those assigned the job.

Our orders were to keep going until we captured a prisoner and as soon as we got one to return. If we did not capture a prisoner, we would have to return to the enemy lines each night until we did. The point where we would attempt this was on the top of a tall, sharply rising mountain called Georgia. Somewhere on this mountain sat some Jerries behind machine guns and in caves. Our job was to go up there at night with a company and snatch one of them out of a foxhole. When I heard this, I was dumbfounded. Who is going to take two hundred men up on that unfamiliar ground in the dark night? Nevertheless, one morning, we received orders to get our weapons in shape and prepare for a combat patrol. That night, as soon as darkness had fallen, the entire company set out on foot for the mountain called Georgia. As soon as we passed through our own lines, our artillery and heavy mortars began to fire upon the Jerry positions. This was the usual procedure every night about this time, so it was nothing to make the Jerries suspicious.

When the artillery fire had stopped, we began advancing up the slope of the hill Georgia in single file with scouts out in the front. Suddenly, the whole company stopped, and a signal was sent back to lie flat on the ground. Then what sounded like three machine guns opened up and tracers, which are bullets that glow like hot irons, zoomed over our heads. I couldn't tell who was firing. Was it the enemy, or was it our guns? We lay there for ten minutes, and word came back that our machine guns were firing, and that this was harassing fire on enemy positions and the regular procedure for this hour of the night. Everyone was quite relieved. We were not sure of our positions and did not know from which direction the fire was coming. The captain and his staff were the ones who planned the route and who knew the way.

After the machine-gun fire had stopped, we started to ascend hill Georgia again. When we were halfway up the hill, the company spread out in fanlike shape. Each platoon was assigned an area over which to advance until contact was made with the enemy. Forward we moved like arms of a giant octopus, searching every corner and crack. The night was a bright one, but the heavy bushes and small trees made the surface of the hill very dark. To make things even worse, the blowing winds swayed the bushes and made them appear to be moving objects. Our platoon had advanced farther ahead than the rest of the company, but we could hear the other platoon, moving over to our left. The first thing I knew I had stumbled upon a barrier constructed of wooden plank and heavy-cut branches. I was about to try to cross this when I caught the movement of a form in the darkness. I looked up, and it was a Jerry. He had no weapon, and he threw up his hands when I pointed my M1 rifle at him. I heard a noise coming from the left, and I froze. I could see from the outline that it was one of the fellows. I whispered, "Don't shoot; it's Nat." The soldier moved forward. Who do you think it was? You are right; it was TS. It looks like everywhere I go, TS is there too. TS pointed his gun at the Jerry. The Jerry raised both hands high and pointed to a cave behind him. He tried to tell us that ten other Jerries were in there asleep. TS said, "Let me toss a grenade in there; that will bring them out."

I said, "No, TS, we have two hundred men spread out on this hill, and if any firing starts, we will shoot up each other in the dark. Our orders were to go until we got one prisoner and then come back. We have got one, so let's get off this mountain."

TS glanced down at the enemy machine gun that was in position a yard to our left and said, "Yeah, I guess there are some more of these babies, sitting around on this hill." At this point, the captured Jerry bent over as if reaching for his ankles. TS stuck the big muzzle of the Browning Automatic Rifle that he was carrying in the Jerry's face and said, "Up, up." The Jerry struggled up, but in five seconds, he was bending over again. "Up, up," cried TS. I pleaded, "Don't shoot him TS, don't shoot." TS and I turned to look toward the earth. The Jerry's shoes were untied, and the guy had been trying to tie his shoes and scaring the daylights out of us. We let the poor guy tie his shoes.

By this time, other men from the company were appearing on the scene. We told them to pass the word back that we had a prisoner and for them to start moving back toward our lines swiftly and quietly. We turned the prisoner over to three fellows, so they could take him down the hill. About six of us remained at the Jerry machine-gun emplacement to make sure that no one would come out of the cave and begin firing upon our withdrawing company. After the company had a three-minute start back down the hill, the rest of us, after cutting some enemy telephone wires, started off the hill. We soon caught up with the company that had halted at the base of the hill. They had not moved on because the captain and several of the men were not there. However, whoever was in command during the captain's absence decided that the main body should move on with the prisoner back to our lines, and that a few men would remain to locate the captain. When we reached the friendly lines, the troops in position were amazed at the fact that we had managed to return with the prisoner and no casualties.

During the walk back to our reserve positions, we were quite proud of our accomplishment as a unit for that night. We had been sent out on a mission to capture a prisoner, and we were back with one. It suddenly dawned upon me that this Jerry must have seen me coming up the hill and could have well shot me. Then I rationalized that he could have been dozing at his guard post, and when he awoke suddenly and saw TS and me, he figured he was surrounded and was too scared to sound an alarm. Maybe the reason the enemy soldier had his shoes untied was he never thought that we would dare trespass upon this mountain. So he grew careless. When we finally got far enough to the rear to find someone who understood the language that the prisoner spoke, we learned that he was not German, but Polish. He said that he had been forced into the enemy army and that is why he surrendered when he saw us coming. We learned also that the captain and the others were safe, and that they had been delayed when they were fired on while searching a house on another section of the hill Georgia. I had recalled hearing a burst of machine-gun fire, but it did not seem too close to where we were, and during the excitement, we had paid it no mind. The prisoner was turned over to intelligence for questioning, and we returned to our reserve positions. Most of the night was spent in joyful kidding about the tension that had existed during the patrol. No one got much sleep that night, but we made up for it the next day.

Our company remained in this reserve position for another week and then moved to a frontline position in an isolated small town high in the mountain. Here, we stayed until the middle of January. Our mission was to hold ground, and we did some light night, patrolling in small groups. Our company did not have any casualties in this town, but Company L had a man killed by enemy fire while on a daylight patrol. The medics covered by the same patrol returned the next day to recover the body of the dead soldier. The patrol stopped twenty-five yards from the body, and the two medics with a stretcher and their red crosses clearly showing, advanced to retrieve the body. When the medics lifted the body to place it on the stretcher, a booby-trap mine that had been attached to the body by the enemy exploded, blowing the dead body and the two medics to pieces. The patrol shocked with what they had just witnessed returned to their lines, swearing vengeance upon any enemy troops they ever got their hands on.

Our next move, after being relieved by the other troops, was to another mountainous section nearer to the coast. We were told to get clean. Shine our boots. Press our pants. Put on our blue scarfs. Look our best. You are going back to the rear. There's going to be a parade. A band will be playing. Soldiers will be marching. Flags will be waving in the air. The general will be present. Awards will be given. Medals will be pinned on chests . . . and you! Yes, you! Our A Scout; Yes, you! Our former A Scout and now our staff sergeant; you will have a Bronze Star Medal pinned on your chest. You will be called a hero. Your folks back home will be proud of you. To me, it seemed and sounded like a pleasant dream. Somehow, I seemed to be floating. It was real, not a dream. It did happen, and my fellow soldiers expressed approval. It was a great moment for me.

The citation read:

> Sergeant, 371st Infantry Regiment. For heroic achievement in action, on 29 December 1944 in Italy. Sergeant, a squad leader, advanced with his company on a mission to capture enemy prisoners. He deployed his squad efficiently in the mountainous terrain and succeeded in working behind enemy positions though the night was clear. Advancing aggressively, he then discovered an enemy soldier that he and another member of his squad immediately captured. The captured enemy yelled a warning that brought heavy hostile machine-gun fire on the squad. His mission accomplished, the sergeant, with the prisoner, successfully withdrew his squad without casualty. His bold aggressiveness inspired the men of his organization.
>
> Entered military service from Washington, D.C.
>
> > Major General, U. S. Army,
> > Commanding
>
> Inscribed on the Bronze Star Medal were the words: "For heroic achievement and meritorious service."

At the end of this glorious day, we returned to our previous mountainous position.

We stayed here until close to midnight February first. Suddenly and unexpectedly, we received orders to pack up and to prepare to move. It wasn't until we had walked over into the flat coastal lands, facing three small enemy held hills that we learned what was up. The division was about to launch a terrific attack that everyone had heard was coming up in the future. We had seen supporting troops moving about to the rear, but we did not know if this was to confuse enemy intelligence or if it were the real thing. At this point, it appeared that the time was ripe. In this flat land, not far from the three enemy held hills, we took up position in a large house. Here, we would remain in reserve to be thrown into the line, if our troops suffered heavy casualties. Dawn would be the signal for the coming battle for our troops.

CHAPTER SEVEN

HILLS X, Y, AND Z

On the early morn of February second, the hillsides of Italy, near the left coast, were rocked and shaken by tons of heavy steel, hurled from cannons and mortar on the ground, and dropped from planes in the air. It was our field artillery, our tanks, our mortars, our airplanes, tearing the enemy to shreds. I thought I could hear the mountains themselves shriek and groan in agony as big chunks of its earth were torn from its surface. This was the morning we were to give Jerry a Sunday punch.

Our battalion was in reserve, and my platoon had been stationed in a large house from which we could get a good view of the mountains before us. The terrific barrage had lifted now, and we knew that the other battalions were launching their attack. We could clearly see the mortar shells exploding on the hillsides and hear the rattle of both American and enemy machine guns. Mixed in with this, we could hear the many short firefights, involving M1 rifles, and occasionally, the sole-racking sound of the feared enemy burp gun. This burp gun fired so rapidly that if one slug hit you, it was almost certain that nine other slugs would also crash into your body.

About mid-morning, two soldiers covered with red clay strolled into the house and said, "We are lost from our company." Our platoon sergeant inquired, "What happened to your company?"

One of the soldiers replied, "Before daybreak this morning, a group of men cleared a path up the side of Hill X through a minefield. They marked the path with white tape so that it could be easily followed. The Jerries listened but did not fire upon the men, clearing the path. While it was still dark and while our artillery was crashing into the other mountains, our battalion started single file up the side of Hill X in the middle of the minefield. The point of the outfit had almost reached the top of Hill X when it struck us. The Jerries began firing machine guns right down the center of the path, and the Jerries artillery struck at the base of the hill where much of the battalion was waiting to start up the path. We only had two choices, either to stay on the path and to get cut to pieces by machine-gun fire or get off the path and risk the minefields. There was no turning back, for the Jerries had sealed off the base of the mountain with terrific artillery and mortar fire. It was mad confusion; the men spread out into the minefield. Some stepped on shoe mines that blew off their feet, just above their ankles, and left them to roll in agony. Some stepped on the 'bouncing-betty' mines. The mine leapt about six feet into the air when the soldier had removed his foot and then exploded, ripping the unsuspecting soldier's body. Others stepped on large mines that tore their bodies into a thousand pieces. We kept walking, and mines kept exploding. The artillery barrage of 88s was so intense that the rest of the battalion had to start through the minefield. Most of them reached the top of the hill and cleared out the remaining enemy troops. In the mad confusion, I found myself wandering around the side of the hill and down into the flat lands from where I had just come. An MP there asked me what outfit I was in, and when I told him, he sent me in the direction of a straggler's area."

The other soldier spoke up, "You couldn't drag me back up on that hill with a bulldozer."

Our platoon sergeant then said, "You, fellows, had better not hang around here. You had better look for your outfit."

As the platoon sergeant left the room, I spoke to the soldiers. "Say, how long have you been in this division?"

"About two weeks," one replied. The other verified the fact.

Then I asked, "Where did you come from?"

The soldier who had done very little talking, spoke up, "I was in a port battalion, loading ships. We had a white officer over us who could never see us as soldiers. All he could see was that he was a white man, and that we were Negroes. He thought we were working for him rather than all of us were working to end the war. I told him what I thought about him one day in a very polite way. He told me that I was one of those 'smart Negroes,' and that he was going to put me someplace where I could get my 'smart brains' blown out. A couple of days later, I was shipped out. I was given two weeks training in an infantry replacement unit, and then I joined this outfit. I was doing okay until this morning on the hill when I saw a guy get his brains blown out. All I could see was that sneering officer saying, 'You are one of those 'smart Negroes.' I am going to put you someplace where you are going to get your 'smart brains' blown out. I am not here to fight; I am here to be punished; they don't care if I help to win this war; all they want is for my "smart brains" to be blown out. Well, it will never happen; I'll sit in prison until I rot."

I didn't ask the two muddy soldiers any more questions. I didn't have the courage or the conviction to tell them they were wrong. I merely wondered how many men were here to be punished because they had dared to express a desire to be treated like men. Fifteen minutes later, the platoon was moving out. We crossed the flat land before us beneath the cover of olive trees. On the way, we passed what had been a temporary aid station and saw bloody bandages strewn about upon the ground. Then we came to the edge of the olive grove. Before us was a clear stretch of land that led to the base of Hill X. In crossing this area, we had to dash and hit the ground several times to avoid sniper fire. After making the last dash to reach the cover of a small house at the base of the hill, I stopped to catch a breath. When I moved around the side of the house, I spied a soldier dressed in his olive-drab uniform. He was propped upon a slanted stonewall almost as if he were standing. He had no face, nothing but a mushy red mass that looked like a watermelon that had been sliced in half. Sudden death must have left him fixed as a horrid warning post. Every man who had come this way had received this shock as he rounded the corner.

Up Hill X, we started; and through the very minefield that the soldiers had described, only we followed the path pointed out by a piece of white ribbon. To the left and right off the path, I could see the huddled forms of men; their packs still upon their backs, who had died from the Jerry machine-gun fire, and those who had stepped upon mines. At the top of the hill, I could see the bodies of the few enemies who had fired the machine guns and directed the 88mms artillery from the rear. Here and there, I could see the foxholes that our men had dug before withdrawing to reorganize. This was no man's land, but we were taking it over.

As we moved around the side of the hill, a Jerry machine gun suddenly opened up from a small house in the valley below. Immediately, a call was made to the 60-mm mortars in the rear. Within ten minutes, two shells struck the house. While the enemy was pinned in the house by mortar fire, a patrol with two BAR teams and five riflemen sneaked in close and laid a withering fire upon the house. The enemy was so occupied that they failed to see a lone American who sneaked in close and threw a grenade in the window. This was the end of another machine-gun nest. Three prisoners were marched from the house as our column of troops spread across the hill. Hill X was ours.

The slaughtered outfit that struck this morning had already removed the poison from the bottle. Our next objective was Hill Y, which was really an extension of Hill X that first leveled off slightly and then rose to form another step in the staircase pattern of mountains. Resistance on Hill Y was slight with only a couple of snipers firing from higher points just to annoy us. Hill Y was ours. The next step in the distance was Hill Z. Before reaching Hill Z, we crossed a shallow depression in single file, taking all possible precautions for any sort of attack. Soon, we were secure upon the crest of the hill.

Although we could not see over the hill, we knew that on the other side was a small town of stone houses in which the Jerries must be entrenched. The first platoon was to sweep to the right of Hill Z, and then into the town. The second platoon to the left of Hill Z, and then into the town. Our platoon, the third, would go over the top of Hill Z, and then down into the same town. Each platoon was to be supported by elements of the fourth platoon, which had mortars and machine guns. The company sat poised waiting for the signal from the captain to strike. Then we heard our heavy artillery coming from our rear; but instead of going over our heads, it began to fall to our rear, and each shell came closer like a walking death. The next shell would be right on us. Everyone dove for cover. This was the one. The ground seemed to shake beneath us. The air became a mass of nothingness, and our eardrums vibrated with such force that our toes did shake. The next shells of walking death continued to march beyond where we lay frozen to the earth and into the town we were about to attack.

The shell that had struck our hill had paralyzed our nerve center. It had scored a direct hit upon our newly established command post. Seven men were hit. Five were dead; the sixth man was not dead; blood streamed from his face and stomach; his legs were a mass of red; he struggled to his feet, holding to the remains of a stonewall for support and cried out, "Water, water, give me water." His lifeblood flowed from him swiftly. He reached for his canteen. He removed the top and took a drink, and then his broken leg bones gave way, pushing through his flesh as they did. He fell sprawled upon the earth. His canteen rolled down the hill, and his poor wretched body gasped his last breath. A pitiful sight that I wished I had never seen. Six were dead. The seventh man hit was the captain. His skull was fractured, and a large hole was in his head. All of his teeth seemed to have been knocked from his mouth, and a large hole was in the back of his shoulder. Several men quickly rushed him off to the rear. The company hastily withdrew back to Hill Y with a few men covering the withdrawal. As I was about to leave, I spied the lieutenant calmly trying to get the smashed radio to work. I said, "Lieutenant, most of the company has withdrawn to Hill Y. Aren't you going?" The lieutenant did not answer. He just kept calling on the phone. "This is Fox Company, the artillery has fallen short, should we move forward? . . . over . . . should we move forward?"

The lieutenant appeared to be so cool as if nothing had happened. I sat on the side of the hill and thought to myself, *Things can't be but so bad, I guess I'll wait here for the lieutenant*. After several more tries, the lieutenant decided that the radio wasn't going to work. He calmly turned to me and said, "Okay, let's go," and we withdrew to Hill Y. That evening, we dug positions and set up a defensive line across Hill Y and waited for the next move.

We spent a jittery night in our mud-filled foxholes, watching, grabbing a nod, and cleaning the mud from our weapons. We heard the Jerries bringing up reinforcements in trucks. They even turned on the headlights once or twice. All of this could have been psychological, but I wondered why our artillery did not blast them. The men were not too worried for they knew that before dawn, we would have reinforcements, and that we would launch a new attack before the Jerries had a chance to reorganize.

The next morning, as day began to break, we peered at one another wondering where were our reinforcements. Why had we received no order to continue on with the attack? They told us that this was a Sunday punch. Now we held the most important point, and it was a matter of continuing on. The division had always cried that it did not get support, and this time, we were promised that we would give a Sunday punch, and that if we took the ground that we now held, that another full division would be thrown into the attack. We had even seen the other troops from a white division moving supplies and men about to our rear. The morning was here. Where were they? Was a psychological game being played? Did the big brass really intend to commit these troops, or was some political game being played? The Jerries knew our lines had been spread thin by casualties. The Jerries knew that we had received no replacements. The Jerries knew that other divisions were not around to give support. The Jerries knew that our side was bluffing, and so they struck. Our artillery did not respond. The Jerries hit our weak-left flank like a ton of bricks. The left flank crumbled, and there was no one to fill the gap. It was merely to withdraw or to remain to be trapped and slaughtered. Smoke shells were lobbed out by the mortars, and with the water cool machine guns laying down a wall of fire, we withdrew down the same path that we had ascended on Hill X and took up positions at the original jumping off point. Oh! How the men did curse. They had won their initial goal and then had been left, sitting ducks. The Jerries didn't dare to follow us for they knew that our fire power on the flat lands was too strong. The flat lands that lay between Hills X, Y, and Z, and our positions in the small hills and farmhouses was once again a no man's land.

The enemy must have felt pretty good; they had regained their lost ground. We felt pretty bad not because of the lost ground but because of the feeling that we had been betrayed. Some politicians in the States and army officers in the rear felt good for we were right back where we started from. They must have shivered in their boots though, for if the attack had been followed through, the division would have received credit for having cracked a strong section of the enemy line. There is no telling how far the attack might have rolled if it had been followed up. A couple of days after this attack, rumors flew that the big brass never anticipated that we would take the ground that we did, and when we succeeded, they dared not push on. We received a small newspaper printed by the armed forces, which stated that our attack was only a limited engagement in which we were merely testing the enemy lines. I thought to myself, *If we make any more tests like that, there won't be anymore around to read about it.* Four days after the February attack, things had become quiet. The Jerries were on their high mountains, looking down, and we were on our smaller mountains, looking up.

CHAPTER EIGHT

NEW CAPTAINS

We knew that the Jerries wouldn't come down out of the hills, so we didn't hang around in this area long. Our company moved back to the positions we held before February first. Our company no longer had a captain since he had been wounded. The lieutenant was in charge, and everyone hoped he would be made the permanent captain. The lieutenant was a great guy. One of the finest fellows I have ever met. I remember one day he was getting some men together for a night patrol. He came to the foxhole where I was staying and said, "Say, Nat, do you want to go on patrol with me tonight?"

I said, "No, sir! I am not volunteering to do anything, but if you give me an order, I'll have to go."

He replied, "Okay, it's an order."

Smiling, I said, "See you tonight." Like I had said, I wasn't volunteering for anything, so I practically asked the lieutenant to make me go. I really didn't want to go, but the lieutenant was a man I would be willing to go almost any place with. Well, that is the way it was with most of the fellows in the company. When I stop to think about it, I just can't think of the name of a single soldier in Company I who didn't like the guy. I can't quite explain it. The lieutenant commanded as much military courtesy as any other officer, but there was just something about him. Whenever you talked with him, he made you feel like you were talking with your brother. I guess the guy had so much respect for other men that you couldn't help but like him. I believe Company I would have followed him to the "burning lands."

Do you think they made the lieutenant the captain? Well, they didn't. They sent us a captain we had never seen before. And he was not a Black captain. I had nothing against the man because he was not Black. He could have been as good a man as our other lieutenant or even better, but our other lieutenant was great in our book, and no one knows better than the men who fought under him. In our eyesight, he was getting a dirty deal, and we resented it. I never had a chance to know our new captain, and I only saw him once. He was with the company for only a short time when I heard that he had stepped on an enemy mine while surveying the area in front of the positions we held. He was killed immediately. Another good man was lost.

The lieutenant whom we liked took over the company again, but within a week's time, we had another new captain. This captain was Colored, and to my surprise, I had seen the guy many years before. When I was a lad, close to my fifteenth year of life, I used to frequent the Police Boy's Club in Washington, D.C. In the building of the clubhouse, there was a room on the third floor, which contained a boxing ring and also many mats for wrestling and tumbling. Our new captain was the man who trained and instructed young boys who wanted to box, wrestle, or tumble. Although I didn't know him personally, I had seen him many times. The new captain was a man with an iron hand. He was so harsh that most of the fellows wanted to rebel against him. He was so bold against the enemy that we often feared that he would get every one killed. The man's courage, which I often thought of as foolish, was so great that he soon became a legend, and we were forced to admire him for his dedication to his country. If any soldier ever seemed to dislike what our new captain said, the new captain would quickly say, "Well, what are you going to do about it, if you don't like what I said, I'll take off my bars, and we'll fight it out." This was a frequent challenge given by our new captain.

It was not strange at all to see our new captain walking around on his hands in the company area or doing some other difficult acrobatic feat. I never saw any of the men in the company accept any of his challenges. I did hear about one soldier who dared his hand. I might add that this soldier had a stomach saturated with alcohol, which probably gave him the needed courage. The soldier had been drinking in the company area and was walking about with a bottle of wine in his hand. The new captain spied the soldier and began to lambast him with harsh words. The captain yelled, "Hey, you, get that bottle down from your mouth, and don't let me catch you drinking in this company area again." The soldier brought the bottle down slowly from his lips and then looked defiantly at the captain. The captain stared the soldier in the eye and said, "If I ever catch you drinking around here again, I'll shoot that bottle out of your mouth." The soldier turned and lifted the bottle toward his lips as though the captain had never spoken. The captain who stood about twenty paces from the soldier reached for his forty-five, and as the mouth of the bottle reached the soldier's lips, the bark of a forty-five rang out. Glass flew in undetermined directions. Wine ran down the soldier's garments. The soldier himself was frozen like a statue with the mouth of the bottle still to his lips, his hand still grasping the neck of the bottle. The rest of the bottle was missing in action. The captain strolled up to the astonished soldier and said, "If you don't like it, I'll take off these bars and this forty-five, and we'll fight it out man to man." The soldier didn't move, he didn't utter a word, and he just stared in amazement. The captain turned his back and walked away. That's the way the story was told.

This was the man who was the new captain of our company for the rest of the war. We later learned that he was a brilliant man in the field of law, for during the month immediately preceeding the war, the captain freed many Negro GIs from all sorts of trumped-up charges and court-martials. Our first move under our new captain was to a point in the higher mountains of Italy that lay midway between the east coast and the west coast. Here, for the first time, we came in contact with fighting units from Brazil. The Brazilians presented a picture that made us feel disappointed. The troops were not segregated because of their color like we were. The units were mixed. White, black, yellow, or red, they all fought and lived together. The officers were men of all shades. The picture that these troops presented set many a mind to wondering. I asked a Brazilian soldier if there was any segregation in the army. He said, "No, there was not." He told me that they never even think about segregation, and he was amazed that such a thing existed in the United States Army.

We stayed here for about a month, and then we moved back to a position on a large hill facing Georgia. It was now the last days of March. The Germans were being crushed on both sides of Europe, and we were preparing to deliver the final blow in Italy. Big guns were being moved into position, and the ranks of all units had been strengthened with replacements. Tomorrow was April 5, and this was to be the day that Jerry would get the works on the Italian left coast.

CHAPTER NINE

THE BIG PUSH

Hades itself could not possibly have been any hotter than were the hills of Italy this early morn in April. Any poor souls that possibly survived the rain of death that now fell upon enemy positions would surely be mindless creatures. There was no bluffing this time. Our side was throwing everything we had. This was to be the clincher. Our regiment was in reserve. Sweeping through our lines, under cover of artillery and mortar fire, was the 442nd Japanese American Infantry Regiment. An outfit whose valor and determination was well known by all fighting outfits. They struck with great fury. One member of a squad would toss a grenade into a cave; and before the sound of the explosion had died, they had charged into the mountainside and had the Jerries running from the caves, screaming for mercy. After a fierce battle, they had won the commanding heights.

At the same time, striking to our right was our sister regiment, the 370th Infantry Regiment that had already been acclaimed for its famed crossing of the Arno River and the capture of Lucca. They stormed into enemy positions to add further confusion to the reeling enemy forces. To make things more miserable for the enemy, a white infantry regiment that had recently been an antiaircraft artillery outfit was thrown into the swirling battle. Within the next two weeks, the whole Italian Front did erupt. The British Eighth Army far over on the right coast launched a bone-crushing attack and just to their left more of the American Fifth Army, and the Brazilian forces drove forward. Our regiment was moved over to the right to a position that was to put us almost in the center of the front. After reaching this position in trucks, we set out headed due north to make contact with the enemy. We walked five miles over small hills and farmlands, but the only sign of the enemy we saw was one dead and bloated body dressed in the uniform of an enemy soldier.

Before us lay a stretch of open land one-mile wide that included a shallow stream of water the width of which was about fifty yards. The column of troops stopped under cover of small brush before entering the clear space. A defense line was set up, and orders were received to dig in. Here we spent the rest of the evening and night.

After this stretch of open land, the earth arose sharply to form a rather steep mountain. On top of the mountain could be seen a large, modern-appearing building that was a hospital. The next morning, a patrol composed of fifteen men and of which I was a member set out on a mission to find the enemy or information of his whereabouts. By now, we were of the opinion that the enemy crushed from both flanks had withdrawn from the whole center of his line to avoid being cut off. We reached the top of the hill after a rather difficult climb to enter the surrounding grounds of the hospital.

The interior of the hospital had been completely stripped of its equipment. The beds were missing, x-ray and laboratory machines had been packed off, and the patients had been moved to the rear. The place was now just an empty shell. There was present; however, three people, two women, and a man. The man was a doctor, and the two women were nurses. The three of them appeared to be complaining bitterly because the hospital had been so severely stripped. These captured medical personnel informed us that the enemy had packed, locked, stocked, and barreled in a hurry and pulled out twelve hours before we arrived at the base of the mountain.

The patrol didn't hesitate here but moved on in the direction of a small mountain town nearby. As we entered the town, the people greeted us with flowers and fresh eggs. Ah, fresh eggs. I had eaten so many powdered and canned eggs that to hold an egg in its shell was almost an unbelievable act. These people also said the enemies were well on their way toward the Po Valley and the Alps.

The patrol moved on over the fifteen miles of beautiful green hillside and slopes, more being downhill than uphill until we were at the outskirts of a rather large town. Here, we were greeted by Italian partisans who were guerrilla troops fighting with the American forces. The leader of the partisans was dressed in a trim green uniform and sported a heavy beard. He was a man of usual size and height. The only thing that attracted your attention was his heavy, dark beard and his peering black eyes. He told the lieutenant in charge of the patrol that his men had captured thirty enemy soldiers and had killed ten out of a group of forty Jerries who had stayed behind as a delaying force. The main force of the enemy had fled a full day ago. I was certainly glad that this partisan group had captured these enemy troops and spared us the woes of running into their waiting ambush. Although the partisan leader mentioned no casualties among his own troops, we knew that he must have lost men, for you do not clear out delaying forces without losing buddies.

After a lengthy conversation with the partisan leader, the lieutenant in charge of our patrol decided that he would enter the town just to look around. As we entered the area of the town, we could see large bomb craters that had been caused by our airpower. In one of the craters were the bodies of two dead horses, that legs extended rigidly in an expression of death. Until that particular moment, the worst odor that I had experienced had been that of a skunk, but this stench of death made the odor of the skunk seemingly pleasant to experience.

After a scanty look about the town, our patrol withdrew from the town and started back in the direction from whence we had just come. Since starting on the patrol, we had covered twenty miles of walking and investigating, and to return would require walking late into the night. The lieutenant in charge of the patrol decided that we would stop in a small town close by that had been suggested by the leader of the partisans, and here we would sleep for the rest of the night.

When we reached the small town, the patrol was split up into groups of fours, and each group of four stayed with an Italian family that had been previously named as trustworthy by the partisans. The Italian couple in whose house I slept that night were very friendly and hospitable. They invited us to dine with them at a meal, consisting of hard-boiled eggs, a sort of paste made from chestnut flour, white hard-rolled bread, and warm milk. Frankly, I was not hungry, but a lieutenant, who was a good friend of mine, insisted that I accept so as not to hurt the feelings of the couple. I struggled through the meal with great discomfort, trying hard and succeeding in drinking the warm milk and eating the hard bread, but it was just utterly impossible for me to put that chestnut paste on top of the warm milk. I was almost certain that if I had, my stomach would have gone into reverse motion, and the results would have been extremely embarrassing. It was indeed a happy moment when the hostess, with a very charming smile, removed the plate from in front of me. That night, we were bedded down in two large extra beds in the house. As usual, we slept with practically all of our clothes on. The next morning, each one of us must have eaten at least a half dozen hard-boiled eggs. A fresh egg was a rarity, and whenever we got the chance, we always ate as many as we could hold. By nine o'clock, the whole patrol had assembled, and with our guts heavy with hard-boiled eggs, we set out for the company area.

Convoy trucks were already present when we got back. The Jerries had withdrawn all the way across the Po Valley and into the Alps, so we had to ride to catch up with them. We rode across the miles of winding hills and through small towns until we found ourselves looking far down into the Po Valley. That late evening, we camped in the area of a farmhouse just outside of a small town. We were now in the flat land of the Po Valley.

Several days later, we heard that the enemy had surrendered to the Allied Armies on our right flank. Within three days, we knew that the enemy in Europe had surrendered to the Allied Forces. This was the day. We had lived through the Italian campaign. Trucks loaded with prisoners began flowing toward Southern Italy from the north. Each soldier of our division received a letter, telling him that the division had done well and contributed much in the defeat of the enemy army. It stated, however, that we now had another job to do in order to defeat the forces of Japan in the Pacific. Before anyone had much time to think about the army of Japan, two atomic bombs had been dropped, and the Japanese forces had surrendered.

For the next month or so, we did guard duty at a prisoner-of-war camp near the southern part of Naples. One of our posts of duty was a small Italian-built hospital that treated wounded enemy prisoners of war. The doctors and nurses were German, but the hospital was supervised by an American headmaster. Our only duties were to prevent the escape of prisoners. Orders were given to us that no one was to enter or leave without a pass.

One day, one of the fellows was on his usual tour of duty at the gate. As he was standing just hoping that his relief would hurry up and come along, a soldier strolled through the gate as if no one was there. The guard said, "Say you have to have a pass to go in there."

The soldier replied, "Yeah, I know it. I work here, don't you see I have on an American uniform."

The guard immediately sensed the soldier was trying to be smart, and he cracked, "Look, I am no mind reader, half the population of Italy is walking around here in GI uniforms. Orders were if you don't have a pass, you don't get in."

The soldier said, "Okay, I forgot it, what do you want to do now?"

The guard replied, "You just step over here, and we will have someone identify you."

At this time the soldier bellowed, "You, n—, think you are running things over here, don't you? Wait until we get you back home." The guard's features in expression of rage contorted themselves in an awesome manner. He reached for his automatic, his whole body rigid with frustration. No man could say that to him, and get away with it. The guard was suddenly shocked to his senses by the harsh voice of the sergeant of the guards, shouting, "Guard!" The soldier, his face blue with fear at the realization he almost got himself shot, turned and walked away into the town. The sergeant continued, "Guard, don't let a fool like that make you waste a good bullet."

The guard said, "I would like to break his neck." Another soldier who had observed the whole incident came down to the gate.

He said, "That fellow has been over here for two months, and he has done nothing but caused trouble."

The sergeant said, "Well, if he starts any trouble when he comes back, we are going to grab him and throw him in the guardhouse. He has his pass because he showed it when he went out of here. Say, Guard, you go over to the guard tent; the fellows are playing pinochle. I'll finish out the rest of the watch."

The guard said, "Okay," and started away; then he turned and said, "Sarge, I'm glad you didn't let me," and he walked away.

The other soldier who had joined them after the incident said, "Gee, I am sorry that—" At this point, the sergeant cut him short.

"Don't apologize for him, that's the way he has been trained, and there are thousands more like him." The sergeant didn't mean to be rude to the soldier to whom he was talking. The soldier sensing too much damage had already been done turned away in a guilty-looking manner and disappeared into the hospital grounds.

The sergeant muttered to himself, *One white man calling you a n—and another one trying to make it up to you.*

Within fifteen minutes, a new guard had arrived to take over the main gate. However, the first guard told the guard who had just arrived that he would wait around a while for the return of a hardhead. Within another hour, the troublesome soldier returned. This time, when the soldier approached the guard at the gate, the soldier had his pass in his hand. The guard took the pass from the soldier and recorded his name on a sheet that contained the name of all who had left and entered during the day. As the soldier stood there waiting for the guard to finish writing his name, he slyly stole a look toward the guard who had been present before. The soldier saw that the guard's eyes were upon him. The soldier seemed quite surprised that nothing had been said to him. Nervously, he clutched his pass when it was returned to him and then started into the grounds. About this time, the soldier realized that he had appeared nervous, and so he threw out his chest, glanced defiantly at the guard, and strolled down the road of the hospital grounds until he had disappeared from sight. The new guard who had just come on duty said to the first guard, "What's the matter with that guy? Is he the hardhead you were talking about?"

The first guard replied, "That's him." Then he explained what had happened.

The new guard standing at the gate said, "Well, I would have thrown him in the guardhouse."

The first guard replied, "Forget about him, the poor fool has one foot in a mental institution. I'll report him to the supervisor of the hospital. Let him discipline him."

We spent two months in this part of Southern Italy, doing guard duty. Then we moved to another prisoner compound to the north and located on the outskirts of the city of Pisa where stands the famous Leaning Tower of Pisa, one of the seven wonders of the world. Here we guarded prisoners of war for two months. During this time, many of the fellows, who had been in the army longer than some of us, were shipped home. The rest of us longed for the time when the remainder of the division would pack up and go home.

One day, we learned that most of us would be shipped out of the 92nd Infantry Division and organized into other units until we were sent home. It wasn't long before this happened, and I found myself with many of my old companions in another area near Pisa, no longer in the 92nd Infantry Division, but now, in a little-known outfit with four numbers such as unit 3215.

CHAPTER TEN

SWITZERLAND AND FRANCE

Yep, we were out of the Nine Deuce as the fellows used to call it. We were now ex-Buffaloes, how our blood boiled. We were burned up. We had often dreamed of the moment when the Nine Deuce, the "Buffaloes," would return to the States and get a grand welcome home. Now the men who had lived through its battles had been shipped out, and other soldiers with longer service, but not true "Buffaloes" were taking their places. Yes, the 92nd Infantry Division was going home, but most of us wouldn't be with it. This unit 3215 outfit was a disorganized sort of thing. It had no definite purpose other than to have some kind of outfit to wait around in. We were the same old buddies, still together . . . waiting to be sent home. The lieutenant in charge told us that arrangements were being made so that some of us could make a tour of Switzerland, and that this tour was being sponsored by the armed forces. Immediately, I jumped at the opportunity and signed up to go. The tour was scheduled to last ten days, and the cost to the soldier would be only thirty-five dollars.

The memory of this trip to Switzerland, I feel will live eternally in my mind as a gratifying experience during my lifetime. Many others who have enjoyed splendor of mountain and lake scenery and its glorious green countryside will also cling to this picture that so inspires that part of man, which thinks, feels, desires, and loves. The train seemed to be winding its way through beautiful meadow and woods, over a tranquil countryside where only the swaying evergreens, the talking pebbles in the brooks, and the resting sight of a shepherd, minding his flock, break the stillness. Truly, a sight for a haven, this land called Switzerland. But it is not the vast beauty of this country that makes it live so vividly in my memory, for a land no matter how beautiful its physical makeup is but a farce if its internal self is not as splendorous. When I speak of a land's internal self, I speak of its people. The people of Switzerland, those who lived on its land were themselves beautiful. No, I am not speaking in terms of looks. I am speaking of beauty in terms of actions. The Swiss peoples' actions made them beautiful; they were kind, gentle, hospitable, good people. These are the things that made its countryside so striking and its atmosphere so peaceful. May this country prosper and forever exist as a living model of men, living together in true brotherhood, and of men who can truly welcome their neighbors. The group that was making the tour of Switzerland was composed of about forty members of the army several of whom were Wacs. My constant companion was another soldier who had formerly been a member of the 92nd Infantry Division and who, like me, had been waiting to go to the States. In glancing about the train, I noticed that two other members of the party were Negroes. In charge of the tour was our guide, who was an elderly gray-haired Swiss gentleman, whose elegant manner and skill disclosed that he had spent most of his life helping strangers to enjoy the Swiss country. We were already calling him Pops.

Our first stop in Switzerland was in the town of Lugano. This quaint town overlooks the clear, sparkling Lake Lugano.

The hotel in which we slept that night was close to the lake's edge, and it was one of the finest hotels of Switzerland and one that wealthy prewar tourists had frequented. From here, we journeyed to the city of Lucerne, which is also located close to a series of crystal lakes. This city is located well within the interior of Switzerland, and everywhere, one could see evidence of Switzerland's great industry—watchmaking. A watch store seemed to be at every corner, and most of our group exhausted the greater part of their funds in the purchases of precious watches.

Our next stop in Switzerland was at a small village known as Sarnen. At the town of Sarnen, the schoolchildren followed me and my companion of a dark hue through the cobbled streets. They were amazed at the sight of men with dark skin. These children had never seen Negroes before; and this, to them, was a rare sight. One of the children asked to touch my companion's face. The child touched my companion's face, and then the child looked at his small hands to see if any of the color had rubbed from my friend's face. When the child saw that the color was real, and not a mask of some sort, he was overjoyed, and the rest of the group of children gathered around the two of us; each child crowding to touch our hands so that they could say that they had done so. A young Swiss man who appeared to be about eighteen years of age and who spoke English well came over to the middle of the cobbled streets where we were surrounded by the children and said, "I'm sorry, these children are worrying you and staring at you so. To see a person of dark hue in this country only happens once in a lifetime." We told the young man that this was all right, and that it was a pleasure to be so admired by his young countrymen. The young Swiss man said, "I will show you about our village." The first place he led us to was Rathaus or town hall. He said, "Switzerland is the oldest true democracy in the world. It began with the formation of the Swiss Federation six hundred years ago. We have, in this country, three thousand independent communities that have been formed into twenty-two cantons. A canton is the same as a state in your country. The first cantons joined together in the year 1291 and the last in the year 1815."

I said to the young Swiss man, "What is the population of this country?"

The young Swiss replied, "We have, in this hilly country, four million happy and prosperous citizens."

My companion then said to the Swiss, "Every place we visit in Switzerland seems to have a different language."

The young Swiss replied, "Yes, in this country, four different languages are spoken—Italian, French, German, and a language known as Bern German."

Then I said to the young Swiss, "Why is it that your citizens get along so well together?"

The Swiss gentleman replied, "It is because we have the democratic idea, which penetrates the confederation, the cantons, and the communities alike. This democratic idea contains an educational principle of a high standard of Swiss popular education. On the other hand, the Swiss popular education embellishes the democratic idea. Each canton and community has its representatives who come together to form a parliament somewhat similar to the congress in your country."

My companion then said to the young Swiss, "We have well witnessed your democratic idea, not just something written on sheepskin, or meaningless words screamed by mouth, we have seen it and experienced it in the wonderful treatment accorded us by your fellow countrymen."

After these words, we bade the young Swiss gentleman good-bye, and we thanked him for his kindness. He replied, "*I am very* glad to have met both of you. You were not at all like many soldiers from America want us to believe." Then the young Swiss extended his hand, which the both of us shook as a token of friendship and left to return to the rest of the group with whom we were touring Switzerland.

As we walked across the cobbled streets to join our group, my companion said, "You know what the young Swiss meant when he said we were not like so many American soldiers want them to believe, don't you."

I said, "Yes, I know some of the other soldiers have been painting derogatory, stereotyped pictures of the Negro soldiers, but the Swiss people are fast learning that they are untruths. I often wonder what sort of opinion these Swiss people have of the other American soldiers when they discovered that they have been spreading lies."

We stopped at many other cities and towns in Switzerland. One of them was a famed tourist town called Interlaken. This town is located between two lakes, and nearby is a tremendous mountain called Jungfraujoch. We visited the Berghaus, Jungfraujoch Hotel, which is known as the House Above the Clouds because it is near the top of this tremendous mountain. In fact, this hotel is over eleven thousand feet above sea level.

The last city that we visited in Switzerland was the city of Neuchâtel, and this city, like the others, was situated close to a clear blue lake. After enjoying the hospitality of this city, we loaded on a train for the last time in this dream land of Switzerland and started to our camps in Italy.

The first news that I received when I got back to camp was that we were leaving by boat for France. The soldiers who told me about this added, "Brother, you are getting on a boat, but you ain't going home."

I said, "France, who wants to go to France? I want to go to Washington, D.C."

The soldier needled me by saying, "I lived in Washington, D.C. for two months and literally detested the place. The nation's capital. The capital of the world's greatest democracy. Everywhere I went, everything I attempted to do, the people seemed so inhumane to their Black citizens."

Every man for some reason likes to take up for his hometown, but I couldn't answer the guy. He was right, and I felt a great sense of sadness. Did he know that I had gone to Washington, D.C.'s Jim Crow schools? Did he know that I had lived in its segregated ghettoes? Did he know I had been denied as a teenager to eat in a hamburger joint because I was Black? Couldn't sleep in its hotels or go to its movies. That Blacks witnessed discrimination in job advancement if employed by the federal government. The Black people couldn't vote. I did not make any comments to the guy. I did have some rather profound thoughts.

This is what I thought. There is one thing I am certain of; I am going back to Washington, D.C. I was born in this city. My family and friends are there. This is my city. I have a God-given right to be there. Yes, I am going back to Washington, D.C. The United States of America is my country too. Washington, D.C., the nation's capital, is my city too. Yes, I am going back. Albeit it, not reluctantly. Yes, I am going back to see it as both a challenge and an opportunity. I'm going back to help make it a place that shows compassion for, humility for, high regard for, and values all of its citizens alike. I looked over at the soldier and said, "When are we supposed to leave?"

He replied, "We are supposed to load on board ship tomorrow afternoon."

The following morning, we packed our personal belongings in our duffle bags. Immediately following the noon meal, the ever-dependable convoy trucks swung into the area, and we clambered on. By five that afternoon, we had loaded aboard a Liberty ship and had set sail for Southern France.

When we pulled into the docks of Marseille, France, early the following night, the first crack we received was from some soldiers who were working on the docks. They wanted to know how things were in the States. Boy, did we burn. To make the men even more evil, we unloaded from the ships and waited around three hours in the damp and cold before anyone found out we were in France. Finally, large trailer trucks arrived, and we took a cold two-hour ride to a camping area. When we reached the camping area, the state of confusion was exhausting; no one knew where we should sleep; our source of food was in doubt and who should be in charge was avoided by all present. The whole group felt like an old dishrag that had been used when it was needed and then tossed aside. We remained in Southern France for two weeks, and then we were put aboard freight trains and shipped across France, toward the northern port of Le Havre. This was a most miserable ride. When we reached the city of Reims, France, we were split up into smaller groups. I was among a group of forty soldiers who were sent to a truck company four miles from Reims. This trucking company was stationed in what appeared to have been a French housing project. We stayed here two months. We didn't do anything important. We just waited around. While I was there, I received an African American newspaper from home. The first thing I read in big red letters was this: The Last of the Famous 92nd Infantry Division Arrives at the Port of New

York. I dashed from barracks to barracks, showing the fellows that we were where we were not.

On the second of December, we left the area just outside of Reims and motored to what is called a staging point located only three miles from the port city, Le Havre, which was a port of debarkation for the good old United States of America. Thousands of troops were already there, waiting for the time to arrive when they were to be sent home. Here I met most of my old buddies from our company that had fought in the 92nd Infantry Division. Among them was my good friend, Sam. It was like old times. We all went to the service club and had coffee together, and many words were spoken of past times. As the days past by much Christmas music was heard about the camp. Loud speakers played pieces like I'll be home for Christmas, and I'm dreaming of a white Christmas. Most of us watched with eager eyes as each truckload of troops left for the port of Le Havre, always hoping that we, too, might leave in time to be home for Christmas. However, the days did come and go, and soon, Christmas of 1945 was a thing of the past. Maybe we could make it home by New Year's Day. Gee, wouldn't that be great, the first New Year's home for most of us in about three years. But time did march on, and the year nineteen hundred and forty-six did come in, and the year nineteen hundred forty-five did go out, but we were still in France.

On the eighteenth day of January, we did kiss the staging area good-bye. We were on our way to the port of Le Havre, France. In short order, I was strolling up a gangplank of a large troops ship with each step seemingly drawing me nearer to the amiable ending of an unhappy dream.

CHAPTER ELEVEN

GOING HOME

If you ask any soldier what moment in his life gave him the greatest thrill, I am about certain he will tell you two words, and they are "going home." For more than a year now, we had waited and wished for the time when we would start the great journey back to the States. The moment had arrived, and a great ship that we were upon was leaving the port of Le Havre, France. Its destination would be New York Harbor.

All eyes had in them a glow of warmth and joy that expressed anticipation of a glorious reunion with family and friends. Visions of old haunts danced before the eyes of many. Yet deeply buried beneath these glows and visions were thoughts of thankfulness that you were making the journey home. The big ship made its first lurch forward; many men silently thanked God for his past protection. In ten days time, we were lining the rail of the ship, gazing with deep satisfaction at the much-heralded Statue of Liberty. Tugboats blared their welcome, and eyes feasted upon the sights of New York Harbor. Within two hours time, we were comfortably settled in Camp Shanks.

That night, we had a wonderful time just enjoying the simple things of life. We went to the post exchange and bought sodas and candy. We looked with great delight upon several Colored girls who worked in the post exchange, for it had been only upon rare occasions that we had been able to enjoy the sight of a Colored girl. To some, it suggested their wives and children; to others, it meant their girlfriends; to another, it brought back the picture of his sister and his whole family life. Several of us left the post exchange and went to a camp movie. Ah, what glorious adventure when you step up and pay your money . . . two tickets appear; you stroll into the lobby, present your tickets, walk in and choose your seat, and then a delightful film of entertainment.

The entire next day was spent in processing before we boarded a train for camps near our homes. By sunset, we had loaded on different trains, and we were on our way to home territory. The train on which I was riding was headed for Fort Meade, Maryland. This was the same camp that I had entered when I was inducted into the army, and it was located about twenty miles from my home town of Washington, D.C. We were at Fort Meade three days. We were given our final army physical and also an opportunity to join the reserves. We also received our final uniform of army clothes. Around noon, I found myself sitting in an auditorium with a ceremony going on, like you have at school graduations. The day was February 2, 1946. At the conclusion of the ceremony, each soldier was given his discharge papers and lapel pin. This was the moment; the fellows burst from the auditorium with shouts of glee; it was over; they were civilians again, plain old jodies. Several large passenger taxicabs were parked close to the building. Several soldiers and I, who were from Washington, dashed to one where the driver was holding open the door and yelling, "Washington, D. C."

We threw our duffle bags into the trunk and piled into the cab that had seating capacity for eight. The driver said, "Citizens, the fare to Washington is two per head."

One soldier said, "Okay, to the White House." The rest nodded approval, and we were off. Back over the same road, many of us had traveled several years ago when drafted into the army. Ah! It was a wonderful ride, with every turn of the wheel, bringing us closer to home. Every drop of burning gasoline carried us closer to our loved ones. The big limousine seemed to float along—like a match stem does on top of the dancing rainwater in a city gutter. In short order, we were passing through Hyattsville. To our right, we saw the small community of North Brentwood, Maryland, and next into Mount Rainier, which was practically an extension of Washington.

All of a sudden, there it was. A big sign saying, "You are now entering Washington, D. C., the nation's capital. Speed limit is twenty-five miles per hour." I looked up at a small signpost on a street corner, and it read: Rhode Island Avenue NE. Good old Rhode Island Avenue. I could have kissed its well-swept streets. I looked around at the happy faces that surrounded me. Some of the men were big; some were small. Some of them were short, and some were tall. Privates, corporals, sergeants, and even a private first class was here. They lived in Northeast, Southeast, Southwest, and Northwest, Washington. Their schooling ranged from the fifth grade through college. Economically, they ranged from the poorest to the well-off. The complexions ranged from black to white. On the shoulder of one was the patch from the Quartermaster Corp. Attached to the shoulder of another was the head of a tiger, which meant that he was from a tank-destroyer outfit. The fellow next to him was a former member of a famous tank outfit that had chased the Germans all the way to Berlin. My eyes couldn't resist settling upon the insignia of the field artillery, the fellows who threw the big stuff. In the front seat was a soldier who had belonged to a port battalion. Two other men wore the patch of the engineers, and I, I proudly wore on my shoulder a buffalo.

All of us had three things in common that crossed our minds. We were all discharged soldiers. We were all Black American soldiers. And as we alighted from the cab at the top of the hill on Rhode Island Avenue, and the mid-afternoon sun shone brightly upon the dome of the United States Capitol in the distance; we all had this same thought, "To you our big fertile country we say; our eyes are wide open. We are looking to see your freedom. Through some twist of fate, we have kept the faith. The road has been long and hard; blood and sweat, death and destruction have been our companions. We are home now though our flame flickers low. Will you fan it with the winds of freedom, or will you smother it with the sands of humiliation? Will it be that we fought for the lesser of two evils? Or is there this freedom and happiness for all men?"

Answer us, our White House! Answer us, our Capitol! Answer us, our Supreme Court! Answer us, our state governments! Answer us, our citizens! Answer us, our big fertile country! Answer us! Answer us!

EPILOGUE

The words "answer us" were written many times out of utter frustration. Sixty years of cold winters, colorful springs, warm summers, and changing falls had rushed by before I penned the first word of the epilogue to *The Buffalo Saga*. This work has been enshrined in my memory. It has haunted my thoughts and has triggered me to raise a new question, "Was it worth the sacrifice?" The outcomes must be magnanimous given the extreme amount of suffering, death, and destruction that had taken place.

The story of *The Buffalo Saga* transcends space and time. What seems like the end is only the beginning. What seems in reality to be ending is in reality endless. When I wrote the words "answer us," they were to questions regarding freedom, happiness, and the lesser of two evils. In retrospect, my thinking at that time was geared toward dramatically improving the conditions that existed for Black Americans. Today, this thinking pales in comparison to the myriad of unmet needs impacting all Americans, if this great country truly aspires to live up to its ideals of life, liberty and the pursuit of happiness for all of its citizens.

While my current thinking is an outgrowth of my war experiences, I am in no way advocating a war as a means to achieve the following goals. The human suffering, death, and destruction of war will not have been in vain if America makes a sincere and sustained thrust at transformation of its thinking, policies, and actions in becoming a more benevolent nation for all of its people and become a major player in helping to bring about peace and harmony among the peoples of the world.

In other words, the bar has been raised. Action needs to be eternal, i.e., for perpetuity. This transformation must have a transfusion of enthusiasm that is infectious and spreads to every leader, every man, every woman, and every child. Its threads must be woven throughout all levels of government, private, charitable, educational, profit, nonprofit institutions, etc. Besides the political transformation required, there are many other critical needs to be considered in a benevolent society, such as safety, education, health care, nutrition, recreation, employment, freedom of speech, respect, kindness, empathy, marriage, companionship, pursuit of happiness, worship, shelter, clothing, transportation, rehabilitation, and belongingness.

Great thinkers have said that "one of the first signs of the readiness for a major 'benevolent thrust' will be signaled by the willingness of the political world to shed its need for prejudice and discrimination." Perhaps, America is demonstrating that it is attempting to do some of this shedding. An African American and a woman were the top-vote receivers in a major party selections in the 2008 primary. A woman was selected by a major party's presidential selection to be a vice president in the 2008 primary. A major political party nominated an African American as its candidate to run for the presidency of the United States of America. This means that America is poised to possibly have an African American as president or a woman as vice president. In any case, we can only have a win-win outcome as either outcome will be of historic importance.

The road has been rocky. The road ahead will have rough spots as well. The dramatic changes in the character of the nations will be the cause for happiness or sadness, stress or relaxation, disappointment or satisfaction, mean-spiritedness or kindness, disgust or approval, deceit or trustworthiness. Hopefully, the final outcome will be benevolence at its best with peace for all nations.

And finally, the connection . . . . The Buffalo Saga, because of its soul and spirit, must and shall for perpetuity be a major player for the thrust for benevolence. May the people of all nations join in this transformation for benevolence. If *The Buffalo Saga* had not been written sixty years ago, then this epilogue would not have been written today.

This Saga is not the only saga to be told by a Buffalo Soldier. For each Buffalo Soldier has a story to tell. All the stories are the same in many ways. On the other hand, all of the stories are different in many ways. No story is the same. Hopefully, more Buffalo Soldier stories will be told.

Signs of progress are emerging. On or about November 4, 2008, an African American was elected as the forty-fourth president of the United States of America, or a woman selected as the vice president of the United States of America.

Moreover, on or about January 20, 2009, an African American took the oath of office and began serving as president of the United States of America, or a woman took the oath of office and began serving as the vice president of the United States of America. One or the other was predestined to happen, so said *The Buffalo Saga.*

It was no longer one or the other. The deed was done. The dye was cast. The outcome was clear. Racism was not a barrier to success.

On January 20, 2009, recorded . . . . in the history of the United States of America . . . . a person of African American descent was sworn in as the forty-fourth president of the United States of America . . . . part of the benevolent thrust.

GOOD NEWS

With the 44th Inaugural, for the first time in the history of this nation, a woman of African descent will become the First Lady of our land. For the first time in the history of this nation, two children of African descent, along with their parents, will live in the White House.

With the 44th Inaugural, our president and congress along with American citizens, continue to discuss the set aside of about one trillion dollars ($1,000,000,000,000) to promote the welfare of our citizens. These are sure signs of part of the Benevolent Thrust as written in The Buffalo Saga.

INDEX

LaVergne, TN USA
12 January 2010
169759LV00002B/3/P